ON BEING A
WIDOW

ON BEING A WIDOW

Helen Thames Raley

WORD BOOKS
PUBLISHER
WACO, TEXAS

ON BEING A WIDOW
By Helen Thames Raley

Copyright © 1980 by Word, Incorporated
4800 W. Waco Drive, Waco, Texas 76703

All Scripture quotations are from the
King James Version of the Bible

ISBN 0-8499-2908-3
Library of Congress Catalog Card Number: 79-67666
Printed in the United States of America

*To all who must endure sorrow
and loneliness, who must accept and adjust
to another life, who must strive for a sense of meaning
and purpose. . . . To all who wait for morning.*

Contents

Preface

LIFE GOES ON, THEY SAY. After my husband's death, I was to wonder how and why.

One day in the summer of 1970, two years after his father's death, I sat with our son, John, in his law office in Ponca City, Oklahoma. He was very much a man now— able, professionally established. There was about him that strength and resoluteness, that fortitude, that had marked his father's life. Apparent in the impressive portrait that dominated the room was the characteristic indomitable courage that had passed from father to son.

John's desk was appointed with the inherited mementos and keepsakes of other years, the familiar JWRs engraved or embossed on every possible surface. John told me of his work, his next court docket, his plans for the future, and how he missed his Dad.

Sitting across the desk in a client's chair, I was aware of a strange immaturity in myself, a dependence, a shifting of our roles. The courage I had begun to assume had somehow been dispelled. As we reminisced over the thirty-five years our family had lived on a college campus, I began to reach over the top of sorrow, even to laugh with John about funny incidents in the President's home where he and his sister, Helen, had lived all their lives.

How quickly the cycle was moving! We spoke of his two sons, and of Helen's daughter. It was time for me to think ahead, my grandmotherhood to be lived in a strange and frightening world.

"Oh, yes," I answered John's questioning look. "They will remember their grandfather, especially the funny, unpredictable things he would say and do."

John looked out the window, high above the street, and across the wheat-country sky, then turned to me, his intense blue eyes squinting in courtroom seriousness.

"Mother, you have really had an interesting life; perhaps these last years with Daddy have been the golden years."

"Yes, you're right," I said. "Those were the deeply satisfying times for your father, the years he realized most of his dreams, not only the ones for the University, but personal dreams for you and Helen.

"For me, there was a brightness in his joy of living, his very presence. . . . It was our own choice world, a sort of mystical Camelot, I think. And it was filled with all the things I want to remember."

"I really wish you would write it down . . ." John began.

"A book?" I took a deep breath. Almost immediately, I was caught up in the idea. . . .

"But John, it would have to be so personal."

And so it is. Never one to cross the bounds of propriety, certainly never to reveal the intimate heartbeats of my life, I am aware that this little book is the difficult sharing of something inexpressible—never intended for public knowledge.

On the other hand, it is my best answer, for now, to three questions asked repeatedly of me over the last ten years:

"How are you feeling?"

"How have you lived through the cutting off from a life literally consumed by your husband and his work?"

"What are you doing today?"

If this book will comfort and inspire another widow whose spirit must rise above the clichés and platitudes; if it will bridge the gap between my world of convention and today's world of unlimited horizons; if it will help someone with a look at practical matters and problems without seeming insensitive or heartless; and if, through the very personal recounting of my experience, it can encourage someone to make another life for herself, to start over, I shall be grateful.

It is spring now. The campus is alive again after a severe winter. Through fresh green, I see the Chapel spire. The house where I live alone wraps its arms around me through busy, fulfilling days, through long, lonely nights. I wait for morning, and when it comes there are the day's appointments, the involvements of an active life.

This is the answer, then, to the three questions. My life goes on. And I must believe that there is no life until one has loved and been loved in return, and that then there is no death.

Helen Thames Raley
Summer, 1978

I

"The Widow of . . ."

"Life is eternal, and love is immortal, and death is only a horizon, and horizon is nothing save the limit of our sight."

PAUL I. WELLMAN

I WOULD HAVE MY EARLY coffee on the north porch where the summer sun slanted through the trees, sweet gums and maples, grown tall now to shade the house. It was just as we had planned, he and I, for our retirement years. Holding my breath for a moment, I sat very still to listen for some sound, to watch for some movement of a living thing, only to realize that I was completely, utterly alone.

Since the death of my husband, who had succumbed to a massive coronary just as life was beginning to be easier for us, I had had no will to live through the bleakness—a future of blank, empty days, one after another. There were times when I could not understand what was happening to me, the quickly changing moods from sudden spurts of bravery to depths of futility. At times I recoiled from reality.

"From now on, you must face it," the doctors had said. "You must realize that he is gone, that you are no longer first with anybody. . . ." That had been the cruel blow, though well-intentioned and softly spoken. This was the facing up to it.

It was well known that my world had collapsed when it happened. He had been so vital, so dynamic, so loving— the light of my life. And I was supposed to be strong, poised, a resilient woman. Everybody expected it of me, but I was somehow unable to handle my grief with the innate dignity and composure that had always been a part of my being.

Dull and unfeeling, I questioned the why of it all. Faith? I seemed to have none. He had always had enough for both of us; with him, I hadn't needed any of my own. The platitudes of condolence I had so carefully written and spoken to others through all the years were meaningless now; the tired clichés only added to my anguish.

For a while, it was like having no name, no identification.

I was to recall many times the very first sentence of Eleanor Roosevelt's appealingly human book of memoirs, *On My Own:* "I rode down in the old cage-like White House elevator that April morning in 1945 with a feeling of melancholy, and I suppose something of an uncertainty, because I was saying goodbye to an unforgettable era and I had given very little thought to the fact that from this day forward I was on my own."

In a very modest way, I felt a similarity of situations. All of my adult life, I had been the wife of a college president, and except for about three years, I had lived on a campus since I entered college at age sixteen.

When elected to the presidency of Oklahoma Baptist University in 1934, my husband, Dr. John Wesley Raley, had been the youngest college president in the United States. Upon his retirement, he had become chancellor, serving four years, then president emeritus for three years—a total of thirty-five years in administration. He had had the distinction of serving the longest tenure among Southern Baptists, the longest in the history of Oklahoma higher education, and the fourth longest in the nation.

From the dust bowl days of the Depression, through war years, and into the colorful decades of Oklahoma's growth and development, Dr. Raley's life had been spent in the dramatic building of OBU. Of the eighteen major buildings constructed during his administration, the magnificent Chapel, bearing his name, had been the last.

The growth of the university during the Raley administration had been reflected in increased property evaluation from $428,000 on June 1, 1934, to $10,000,000 at the time of his retirement from the presidency twenty-seven years later. Accreditation and increased endowment had also marked his tenure, the enrollment keeping pace in expanding programs from less than 300 to 1500.

In the foreword of *The Golden Days and the Gallant Hours* (1974) our son, John W. Raley, Jr., characterized his father as "the most adventurous man I have ever known. Possessed of an unquenchable longing to see beyond each horizon, he had an optimism and belief that each new dawn brought an ever better day. His small stature cast a shadow of gigantic proportions, touching the lives of thousands, yet he was the gentlest of fathers."

Upon the dedication of the Chapel, 1962, our daughter, Helen Raley Nash, said this: "My father, demonstrating his resilience in the face of every obstacle, is optimistic and independent in spirit. He thinks on a grand scale, fights for his convictions, and settles for nothing but the best. For John and me to grow up sharing such rich experiences is a wondrous heritage."

This, then, was the man who had chosen me to spend life with him. Oklahoma Baptist University, of course, had been our job, our obsession. There had never been any doubt about it; Dr. Raley's work was mine too. Our name, our family, our home had been synonymous with the university. In spite of disappointments, distressing problems, and often despair, life had been one glorious adventure in love and loyalty, and in dreams.

My name, his name, was important to me, now more than ever. (Although I began eventually to use my legal identification for publication purposes, I remain, in introductory remarks and editorial comments, "the widow of . . ." I like it that way.) He had given me confidence and approval, even adulation, in whatever feeble efforts I made. I respected his judgment. To pick up a conversation, to smooth over some inadvertent remark, to encourage my cause, all these securities had been mine. I never doubted his dependability to be there when I needed him.

Then, on May 21, 1968, the flags had flown at half-mast on the campus and on all public buildings downtown. The Chapel flags had been draped in black, the service broadcast and telecast. People from all walks of life had come to the Chapel and filed past the bier for hours—silent tribute from students, faculty, and hundreds of religious, political, and business leaders from across the South.

And I was on my own. How could I, in this lostness, become my own person, achieve identity? How could I live effectively without him?

Often, during this time, I thought about my Grandmother Hodges, who had been in mourning as far back as I can remember. She seldom appeared in public, and except for an occasional drive in the back seat of the family car, she never left her world, my childhood home. There was always a faraway look in her eyes, and she never wore color.

Everyday clothes were in gray—long, full "Mother Hubbard" style dresses in gingham or fine chambray, with high button collars and long sleeves. On Sundays, or for special occasions, she wore black silk, made from the same pattern but with a white lace collar set off with an onyx brooch in a modest gold frame. There was no other ornamentation except her wide gold wedding ring.

Old Mama never sang in church when we took her once a year to an evening of the summer revival, but her face reflected a kind of peaceful resignation as the old hymns replaced the rollicking evangelistic tunes. Sometimes she sang snatches of hymns—"Rock of Ages," "At the Cross"—to herself as she rocked on our front porch on summer afternoons.

These little bits of hymn-singing were momentary, however. She was at her best when she reverted to the younger, happier days when Old Papa had come home safe from the War between the States. Then she would sing quite lustily his favorites, "Juanita," and "We're Tenting Tonight on the Old Camp Ground."

My grandmother had lived through Comanche raids, escaping once with a baby in her arms to the woods as far from the house as she could run. She had stood gallantly with the few faithful slaves (my grandfather away with the Confederate Army) as Yankees came to confiscate more than one hundred bales of cotton to be shipped north from the plantation. But she never fully took up life again after my grandfather's death. When the disposition of home and

land was complete, my grandmother became a member of
her children's households, as was the custom of the day,
the accepted thing to do.

We, who remember ever so faintly, must have been
touched, even as little children, by a respect for her grief
and for her widowhood which she wore with such dignity
and grace.

Even as times and customs changed, deceased members
of my family had always been mourned through a respect-
ful period of time and with a reluctance to pick up life
again as though nothing had happened. We felt things
deeply.

Now, in my own grief, I seemed to have reverted to the
old ways, disclaiming the attitude of going right on with
living. I simply had to stop for a while.

Is it true, as someone said, that the opposite of love is not
hate, but withdrawal? Reaching out in desperate need for
something to assuage my bitterness, I could only draw
back into a walled-in seclusion.

It never occurred to me not to observe a period of
mourning. The thought of going out socially, of attending
club meetings, of being seen at public occasions was
unthinkable. Gradually, I tried to attend church, always
choosing a spot out of sight of our family pew because it
only reminded me that life would never be the same. As
though sensitive little antennae were catching every vibra-
tion, I would shudder when I heard a certain strain of
music, a bit of poetry, a familiar voice. All comfort seemed
to elude me.

Because my public life had been cut off completely, the
way to begin on my own was incomprehensible. I identify
with Mrs. Roosevelt as she told of her fright, her feelings

of inadequacy and uselessness after the President was gone. Her "image," however, remained; she often felt that too much was expected of her. But, according to her biographer (Joseph P. Lash, *Eleanor: The Alone Years*), she regained her confidence, her stature, and eventually "turned her sorrow into a strengthening thing."

Through the pain, I learned that one does what has to be done. Straight ahead, behind dark glasses, I too began the long way back into reality.

In my own way, and surely this is the prerogative of every woman who mourns, I began to organize the responsibilities at hand. Some had to be met immediately. When I couldn't even think, it was necessary to give information, funeral details, lists and data to the press. Personal choices, those deeply hurting decisions, were made easier by the funeral director, a family friend, whose gentle guidance led me into some reality. Telephone calls were put through carefully and kindly. Under stress, one makes unfortunate decisions, but in retrospect there are only a few regrets.

At such a time friends become family, close and supportive. In conventional ways, we were remembered— with food and flowers, calls and telegrams. Condolence cards were stacked in large cartons to be read in succeeding months, later to be bound. For many years, memorial gifts were to be processed.

Notes and mail were left at the door; necessary purchases were delivered. Given every courtesy of privacy, I checked and rechecked the safety-deposit box, following directions through confusing legalities, signing my name over and over on documents and certificates. Housekeeping routine provided a welcome tiredness. The days began to go by in the organization of the hours, although the endless nights were endured only with the thought that morning would come.

It was then that I drove out to Resthaven, the Memorial Park—green and misty like the English countryside in the spring and summer gently rolling toward the Thames. The vigils were mine to keep alone, and although I was criticized for their frequency, I was being restored there in a strange, quiet peace.

If I could have shared this grief, I am told, it might have been less painful. But I was the one to hold it close. It was so personal; I wanted no intrusion. My way of coping might be considered strange, abnormal, unorthodox, even un-Christian. Some thought it was unhealthy. But it was the only thing I could do.

The writing helped most, approximately 1500 handwritten letters completed in two months to acknowledge the expressions of sympathy. An unfinished manuscript was taken up again, revisions and additions filling my mornings. I remember that there was autumn in the air, a crispness of vitality in that familiar feeling that school would start soon. At times, I could hear his voice, the resonance and buoyancy enveloping me as I looked north from the porch. It was still clear, vibrant, and mellow— "The haze on the far horizon, the infinite tender sky"—I had heard in so many autumns of our life together.

As though by some designed directive, a most unusual television program one evening prodded my thinking about being the widow of a great man. Eric Sevareid's "Conversation with Mrs. Charles A. Lindbergh," commemorating the fiftieth anniversary of the flight to Paris, was an inspiring, unforgettable production.

Early in the program, I realized that Mrs. Lindbergh and I shared similar experiences related to Lucky Lindy and his fantastic flight. When Mr. Sevareid asked about her knowledge of the 1927 venture, Mrs. Lindbergh admitted that she hadn't known who he was, and on that particular day when he had landed at Le Bourget Field, Paris, she had been in the basement of the college library working on a term paper, and had known nothing about such a spectacular event. Nor had I, for I had been involved in college finals. Not until I had gone home for summer vacation and had time to read the newspapers my mother had saved for me, had I known anything about such a daredevil stunt.

Clear-voiced and at times vivacious, Anne Morrow Lindbergh charmed the television audience with both propriety and candor. In her face there were lines of good humor, and yet the sadness of one who has seen great tragedy. She seemed an amazing mixture of superlative strength and a sort of mystical femininity; her serenity was inspiring.

"He expected me to fly with him," she said. "I had to learn the Morse code and was responsible for the radio. You see, I was his contact with the world wherever we flew."

And in one suspended moment, when asked about the controversy in their younger days, she said for all the world to know, "Fame is a sort of death." In a sense, she had always been "the widow of . . ."

Quietly, Mrs. Lindbergh spoke as she had written, about the ebb and flow of life, the variables, the intermittences, the periods of change, and how all these contribute to one's creative sight and understanding.

When asked how Col. Lindbergh had faced the inevitable, how he had made arrangements to return to Hawaii for his last days, she quoted his statement: "I have faced death many times, but until now, there was always something I could do. . . . Now, it isn't something to face. . . . It is harder for you, watching, than it is for me." This was indeed the spirit of the Lone Eagle.

Mrs. Lindbergh continued, "It is very difficult to be a widow. When a man dies, it is like a tree falling. One sees the whole length of life at first, then gradually the periods of that life. For my husband, there were three distinct eras: aviation, efforts to keep us out of war, and then his obsession to improve the quality of life around him. . . .

I listened carefully as she spoke of periods of change in our lives and how they can be creative "if you are strong enough." It was then that I remembered something she had written almost prophetically as a much younger woman: "It isn't for the moment that you are struck that you need courage, but for the long uphill climb."

After so many years, I was there, still there, grudgingly plodding that uphill climb. But strangely, somehow, I began to feel a living, thriving, immortality, a life-goes-on pattern. It was something real, reasonable, and almost touchable.

This experience is shared with many women who were a part of their husbands' identities, perhaps a part of whatever success their husbands might have achieved. There was, and always will be, a sort of a basking in his glory. The image is inescapable.

Being the widow of a strong man who was President of the United States is certainly not the whole story of Eleanor Roosevelt, nor of Lady Bird Johnson, who strives, she says, to "balance her role as the widow of . . ." with a new process of discovering herself. That has meant "picking up those things that were purely for her own pleasure, things she had long since laid aside."

I was to learn that, although widowhood presents a woman sometimes as a nonperson, or a half-person, she need not succumb to the hopeless abandonment of life. Nor need she forfeit, for any reason, the identity she once shared with her husband. Awareness of this is a way toward selfhood, a disciplined motivation, and a measure of contentment.

For security, and even a bit of happiness, I am on my own. I must make my own way.

He left me just enough faith to try.

II

The Miracle of Memory

"How lucky we are to have such a treasure of memories."

MRS. LYNDON B. JOHNSON
(from personal correspondance)

THROUGH THE CHANGING of the seasons, after the spring I could not focus into reality, the lostness prevailed. The Chapel clock, high in the tower, seemed to have stopped. Thoughtful friends had returned to their own responsibilities; the children, caring and loving but busy with all the obligations of their generation, had picked up their lives again.

And now, it was summer again. Again I sat on the porch. And in the backyard, the world waked.

A mockingbird swooped off her nest in the honeysuckle.

A terrapin ambled through the petunia bed.

The paperboy came; the mailbox clicked.

The day began, and there were things to do. I must get to the kitchen. With an effort toward courage, I lingered at the breakfast table, the other chair where I could touch it.

But when the telephone rang, my voice was steady.

"I'm going home," I replied to the voice that asked about my plans.

Quickly, I had made up my mind. I was conscious of a decisive step. I must go home, back to my childhood home. Perhaps there was something there, something I had left so many years ago. Perhaps I could be a child again, revisit all-but-forgotten places, walk along familiar trails, recall young dreams.

I know that many have tried this, and that they say it's never the same. Disappointed, disillusioned by the common sense of maturity, the inevitable shrinking of dimensions, one usually finds he can't go back. But I must try!

It was a bright summer day, hot and still. For several hours I had driven south, exiting the Interstate at Austin and angling cross-country on a fine farm-to-market road, up and over the rolling hills, through the lost pines of Texas, and now over the new bridge into Smithville. Lowlying gulf clouds diffused the brightness of midmorning.

My directions momentarily lost in a new traffic pattern, I eased up to the stop light on Main Street. I felt an excitement, an anticipation, when I recognized Haynie's Grocery and Trousdale's Drug Store on opposite corners just like they had always been. Two blocks down the street was the town's landmark, the great white-columned mansion where several generations of landowners had created a dynasty in cotton. This was home. I could feel it.

In a pleasant nostalgia, I parked the car in Papa's old parking place across from the bank, in front of Hill's Dry Goods Store where Mama used to do her shopping. The high curb scraped the bumper in the same old way.

From this vantage point, the years rolled away. I was a little girl again, sitting on the running board of the car to eat an ice cream cone Papa had bought me. In retrospect, it seemed a simpler, kinder time in a plain, old-fashioned place. And that's where I had left my childhood.

Back to the traffic circle, I found the familiar turn, past the gin and the cotton mill, and up over the hump of the railroad track (obscured now by high weeds and grass), along Gazley Creek, and on to the cemetery road. Polly's house looked just the same.

"Baby, is that you?" she answered my call in her high-pitched voice from the backyard where she was hanging her washing on the clothesline.

After all these years, she recognized my voice.

"I's coming, Honey . . ." I could hear her through the rusty screen door.

Slowly now, shading her eyes with her hand, she padded around the corner of the house, her skirt hiked up over her thin, brown legs, her old bedroom slippers run-over and flapping. A ragged cook apron, faded-out blue, and damp from the washboard, swathed her waddling figure. In contrast, a recently acquired scarf of brilliant, psychedelic colors covered her crinkly gray sprigs of hair.

Unbelieving, but jubilant, Polly put her arms around me and hugged me tight.

As far back as I can remember, Aunt Ellen and Uncle Ned, Polly's mother and father, had been a part of our farm home, faithful Negro "retainers" of another era. Aunt Ellen had always been there in the kitchen to cook on special days, to do the washing and ironing, and to supervise fall and spring housecleaning. Uncle Ned, handyman, had worked the garden and the orchard, plowed a little, cut and stacked the wood. His special forte had been to keep the fire going around the washpot on hog-killing days, and to help render the lard.

Polly, a part of my childhood, had been eight years old when I was born. Self-appointed nursemaid, she had taken charge of my first years, her grandest hours spent wheeling me round and round the yard in my big white wicker buggy. Later, we played together as best friends.

For quite a while, we sat there on the shaky old steps she had propped up with bricks. The summer's heat had dried up a patch of faded petunias at the gate. On the edge of the sagging porch, a wispy fern grew in an old tin bucket. One of Mama's discarded rocking chairs stood just inside the door.

For a moment I was home again, no longer lost, no longer bereft, but safe in the years of my childhood. It was the view south, the ageless trees rimming the top of the hill, that reminded me of all the years in between, and of my place now in the irrevocable design.

"Yo' Mama and yo' Papa both out there now, Baby. It's a pretty place. Go see for yo'self, and you'll feel better."

And then we talked of all the changes in her world and mine. I told her about the children, and their children.

"I sho' can't think of you being by yo'self. It was in the paper, the man at the store tol' me. I wish I had a picture of that big buildin' with Mr. Wesley's name wrote across the top," she drifted off, thinking.

Then, "Is Miss Helen's little girl like her mama that time you brung her home?"

"Yes, Polly, she's very much like her, a very special little girl. Now, I must go on to the cemetery," I said, thinking of flowers wilting in the car. "Must hurry before it gets so hot."

It didn't take long to drive to the top of the hill, to turn left into the quiet lanes of gray marble. Cedar trees Mama and Papa had transplanted years ago, now grown tall, shaded the family plot. What a gathering there was—so many of the family. And there was Old Mama, peaceful now that the war she remembered best was over.

Lingering there in the quietness, I gathered up the people, the places, the little fragments, the little episodes of another time. From the hill, I looked over the fields of my childhood, a vista toward "things not seen" which neither time nor distance would erase.

In the hovering haze of summer, the valley enfolded the town, the river. There was hardly a sound anywhere, only the faint hum of cars on the Austin highway.

I listened for the noon train, just as I used to do. Mama had always said the sound made her lonesome. It was like a dove's mournful call when we lived on the farm.

Across the river, I could see the tall windmill that marked our farm. Cotton fields in the distance, no longer cultivated, had been turned into grazing land for the cattle.

I wondered whether the cotton mill whistle had blown that morning at six o'clock, and whether the Catholic church bell had tolled at seven.

There were a few familiar outlines. To the old red brick school building, all but hidden now by the trees, temporary rooms had been added. The churches seemed to be on the same corners.

There was a new City Hall, contemporary in style, functional, they said, and I could see the flag.

One of the river mansions had been cited by the Texas Preservation Society; another had been turned into a convalescent home.

The new high school was on the edge of town, out toward the drive-ins, the barbecue stands, and a miniature suburbia.

Distances were shorter now, but it was the same town.

Deep are these roots, inescapable, restorative. From them, life goes on, generation after generation. Perhaps the past is really never gone, always a part of the present.

Far beyond the world of my childhood is the far-flung dimension of speed and space; beyond the bourn of quiet, simple things are the complexities of contemporary living. But the eternal verities remain as they were. I found them again: the memory of home and family, of respect and dignity, of work and diligence, of order and loyalty, and—always—love. And I found an immortality I could understand.

On the way back to town, I waved and called out to Polly. She was still sitting on the steps, resting, she would say, and remembering. . . .

And I too remembered. In a way I had come full circle, a long way back home. In that miracle of memory, the scattered pieces fell into place.

So long ago, that Scotch-Irish preacher, short of stature, strong in spirit, and destined to become a college president, had chosen me to share a life far beyond my girlhood dreams. His enthusiasm for living, his amazing energy toward a life purpose, had become mine too.

Ever the paradox, he was tender, but tough when he had to be; poetic, yet practical and down to earth. An idealist, he was also a realist and a pragmatist. Tempestuous, intemperate, impulsive, he was also steady as a rock—and as inflexible. Unquestioned integrity, dauntless courage, indomitable will—these attributes characterized the man. With him, I had known a full and rewarding life, never perfect, but satisfying and secure, idyllic, and destined.

Involuntarily, I headed back toward that life. Main Street now, then west, over the bridge north, and I was on my way. There was a strengthening, a determination, a deep, deep breath.

In my resolution, I remembered the Victor Hugo lines about the bird, resting momentarily there on the bough, then flying on, "for he knoweth he hath wings."

III

Adjustment—Acceptance

"When the joy of living is lost, O God, and life becomes a long weariness, kindle again the light that has failed, and the love that will not let me go."

A PRAYER

I REMEMBER IT NOW. I was radiant with happiness, a glowing bride of only a few weeks.

Dr. Raley was on his way to conduct the funeral service for a friend; I had made some excuse not to go. At the door, he turned to me and said very gently, "One of these days, you're going to have to accept the fact of death, for after all, death is a part of life."

Later, he explained it this way, "In loving, you and I assume the risk of loss. Don't be sad or morbid. It's just that you have always been protected from grief. We're so happy now, but we must accept the fact that one of us will have to live without the other some day."

And then, he quoted the Elizabeth Barrett Browning line: "Unless you can swear for life or death, oh fear to call it loving."

Through succeeding years, there were sorrows. We gave up parents and friends; many students became gold stars during the war. But he was always with me.

We had been married for most of my life when he said

one day, naturally and almost casually, in a conversation, "If anything happens to me, you are going to adjust to it, and accept it."

Caught off-guard, and somewhat disconcerted, I dared not even think of such a thing. I even left the room, as unwilling to discuss death then as I had been in those younger years of our marriage. I positively would not allow any thought of widowhood. As for being prepared, I thought that there was plenty of time to think about that later. Not now, I told myself.

When it did happen, grief tore me into little pieces. Every step of the procedure hurt—from the arrival of the ambulance on the first fateful night, through all the connotations of finality. I remember the resistance to pain, the fighting back. There was no place to hide until it was all over, no cleft in the rock, no surcease nor balm for the throbbing ache.

At the same time, there were decisions to be made. Those last selections, all the proprieties of funeral customs were pushed into my mind with dispatch. Checking figures on the plot, the casket, the marker, the services, and all such excruciating details required more care and courage than I could muster.

In our society, three people, usually male, figure in a widow's decisions—the minister, the funeral director, and the legal advisor. All too often, the widow is at the mercy of untrustworthy advisors. She becomes wary and fearful of unscrupulous dealings at a time when she most needs mental and emotional equilibrium.

I was fortunate in having sympathetic, interested friends to perform these roles. Having a son who was a lawyer was a decided advantage to me. And a letter, addressed to John and providing "instructions and arrangements" had, I now know, been in the lockbox a long time.

But I was still faced with the knowledge that, in all these matters, I had the last word. There was something disrespectful, I kept thinking, about all those copies of the death certificate and the filing of insurance claims, while writing checks and paying for "services rendered" was an assumption of authority I did not want.

It was when I faced the cancellation of my husband's schedule of speaking engagements and travel reservations that the finality became real to me. Later, to see his name marked with an asterisk, denoting "deceased" on rosters of trustees and directors, honorary memberships, to say nothing of calls and mail directed to him, defied my every effort toward resoluteness.

Nothing, of course, in a widow's experience is as traumatic as the disposition of personal effects. For me, Dr. Raley's personality was vividly reflected in the clothes and accessories. I remembered his fondness for British tweeds, too hot and heavy for Oklahoma weather but worn with the flair of Bond and Regent Streets, London. The Hong Kong silk suits, the monogrammed shirts, dared a touch a luxury after the pitifully limited wardrobe of younger years. The evening clothes, the loud plaid sports jackets, all characterized a man with boundless energy for living. The brocaded vests for holiday wearing brought back happy memories. The shoes, in all stages of wear, had covered a lot of miles. The last-used toiletries I touched again wistfully; the fishing gear broke my heart. When his car was driven off, I thought I would die.

As to the books in our personal library, they were to

remain as they were last used, at least for a while. Weeks passed when I never touched them, nor came near the desk where he had worked.

I can say that to "get everything, every reminder, out of the house" is not an easy, clean-sweeping process. It takes weeks, months, and sometimes years. Objects and feelings linger; an atmosphere hovers, and yet so much has slipped away. Reality is painful.

Many of my widowed friends report experiencing the same plight as I—feeling lost and confused while trying to cope with unfamiliar situations. Conversations reveal common thoughts: "without warning," "we never discussed death," "he always seemed indestructible," "he was never sick," "I am so frightened," "I know nothing about business," "our children are too busy," "there was no time to prepare," "we avoided the thought of his going" . . .

At best, a widow is faced with difficult, often insoluble, problems. Mr. Hugh C. Sherwood, in a *Harper's Bazaar* article, suggests that much of the difficulty can be alleviated by advance preparation:

"A death in a family is an agonizing time for everyone, with a multitude of things to do, all requiring attention under the worst possible emotional circumstances. A properly prepared letter of instruction will give the survivor of the deceased access to much-needed information. In addition, it provides an informal, cost-free way of managing one's affairs while alive. . . . Widows are often unaware of the simplest matters, where their husband's will is, or his life insurance policy, or the title to the car. . . . Be sure the letter includes a list of advisors to whom you can turn for counsel if your husband dies."

Mr. Sherwood makes these practical suggestions, advising that the information should be available and accessible to members of the family:

I.   Assets
     A.   Life insurance
     B.   Benefits
     C.   Social Security
     D.   Other sources

II. To Do First
     A.   Arrangements with funeral home
     B.   Vital statistics required
          1.   Birth and birthplace
          2.   Father's and mother's names and birthplaces
          3.   Length of residence in state
          4.   Military service, if any, and dates
     C.   Social Security number
     D.   Insurance policies and numbers
     E.   Cemetery plot and deed
     F.   Necessary copies of death certificate
     G.   All necessary information for medical, car, home and household, accident insurance
     H.   Notification to bank, if necessary, about mortgage arrangements

III. Personal Papers
     A.   Will
     B.   Birth certificate
     C.   School and college diplomas
     D.   Marriage certificate
     E.   Military records, if any

   IV. Bank Accounts, Savings and Checking, and Numbers (Locate canceled checks and bank statements for preceding year)

    V. Income Tax Returns
      A. Location of previous records
      B. Tax accountant—name, address, telephone

   VI. Safety-Deposit Box
      A. Bank
      B. Key
      C. Contents

  VII. Credit Cards (List all cards to be canceled or converted to another name)

 VIII. Stocks, Bonds, Certificates (List all pertinent information, including numbers and maturity dates)

   IX. Car (Locate registration papers, list necessary information on maintenance of vehicle)

    X. House
      A. Insurance
      B. Inventories of furnishings
      C. Mortgage, abstracts, etc.*

Although it is a tedious chore, it is advised that such a letter of instruction should be updated every year, or as circumstances change. A copy, of course, should be directed to one's lawyer.

*Huge C. Sherwood, "What Every Woman Should Know About Her Husband's Estate," *Harper's Bazaar*, November 1974, p. 105.

There is much to be said for putting one's house in order, figuratively speaking, and for clearing out the clutter that distracts and diminishes one's efficiency. For many widows, this is an exercise in decision, in closing chapters, and in establishing priorities. A small desk file, a lockbox, a safety-deposit box at the bank are indispensable. A discipline to write everything down, to keep every receipt or canceled check, becomes a way of life.

The process of learning to handle such matters, of adjusting to my new life, was a slow and painful one for me. Gradually, as I began to face the reality of adjustment—and life is, I have learned, a series of adjustments to various situations—I also began the burdensome process of acceptance. So adjustment and acceptance for me were simultaneous. Both experiences evolved slowly toward some reasonable pattern of living. Ecstatic happiness would never return, I knew, but I prayed for some consolation, some release from the resentment—for peace of mind. And I wondered whether I would ever be whole again.

How I have wished to be valiant like so many who have had to start over as though nothing had happened. Life goes on, they say, and they can take whatever cards are dealt. There are others who fight with the only weapon they have, a daring flamboyancy, although in time their bravado becomes a pathetic façade.

Between these two extremes, most of us trudge along, trying to adjust and to accept. Among my widowed friends, there were several who faced resolutely, head-on, all the problems with a determination to chart a new course as soon as possible. Some could not afford to miss a day's pay; a few went back to school to prepare for a career; one or two moved away, completely changing scenes. Some faced a drastic decline in their standard of living, selling nonessentials and moving into cheaper housing. Most got back into their activities with only a short break. Only a few were unable to face the world.

For all, there was fear, the fear of reality.

Each had to start somewhere, the first step alone. The first little efforts toward normal living, if only a trip to the grocery store with a short list, are often regressive. We try again.

At some points, moments of courage last longer.

Locked-in feelings creep around the edges of articulation.

Finally, a day without tears is a triumph.

I can look back now to realize that, after the first year, my pain was less acute. In handling practical matters, I began to feel more confident and independent, and I soon made the decision that, although I would rely on John for legal questions, I would never try to impose on either child those problems I could handle myself.

There were times when the way ahead seemed possible, even logical, but often the day-by-day steps were frustrating and depressing. At times I was bemused by the glib suggestions about "building a life of your own," "having your own career . . . it's about time," "making the most of the years ahead," and—the most heartening of all—"age has nothing to do with it. . . . You're still young!" I took hope, and loved the vote of confidence—once in a while!

Meanwhile, I was groping through the labyrinths of contemporary thought on what it means to be a woman. Jane Howard, in her book, *A Different Woman*, refers to the inescapable wave of feminism as something to be reckoned with and claimed as healthy and constructive. Was it just a fad, or the wave of the future? Were there really new worlds for me, for every woman, to conquer?

How could I ever adjust to such ideas when I was dismayed even by the strange-sounding, multisyllabled rhetoric? Women today speak a new language—relatedness, interaction, psychotherapeutic encounters, transactional relativity, transcendental and experimental episodes, ethnocentricity, margination, admixture of analytical processes . . . and whatever! Translated, this all means we are living in a very different world from the one in which I grew up. And every woman, whether or not she is aware of it, is a part of the changing scene.

Once, when I was very young, I visited briefly with Dorothy Dix as she rocked placidly on the stone veranda of Grove Park Inn in Asheville, North Carolina. It had been she who had pioneered the humanizing of American journalism. Coming on the scene at exactly the right time, she had helped her generation find answers to increasing social problems. I wish now that I could have asked her one more question: could she look down the years to the potential, the independent spirit of today's new woman? Could she anticipate the resourcefulness needed to cope with life in a new century? What of succeeding generations?

Despite the changes, I believe most women are still looking for answers to the same old questions: fear, insecurity, and loneliness. I doubt seriously if the "new woman" syndrome can alleviate the problem, for many of us in the older generation were born into and grew up in the wife-mother-homemaker pattern, time-honored and revered as the choicest career for a woman. Even now, in changing times, 95 percent choose marriage as the ideal lifestyle.

To me, marriage represented the highest fulfillment; to be a part of my husband's career added a dimension of special favor and position. When that was taken away from me, nothing satisfied. At first, I felt abandoned, discarded. Futility prevailed against all the therapeutic measures, all the tricks and emotional crutches, and the tranquilizers, and all those miserable platitudes.

I realize now that this happens to any woman who has been safely cherished until some great tragedy eventually reveals those qualities imperative to survival. The unexplored places of one's soul are finally exposed, every asset recruited, every resource employed. Lauren Bacall was right when she said that being a woman is a fight all the way—this is true regardless of what one thinks of the feminist movement and the rise of the "new woman."

Be that as it may, most women need a man around the house—for love and companionship, security, support, and just general "know-how." Like many women who live alone, I have fought that helpless desperation that comes when do-it-yourself doesn't work. My difficulty in handling the simplest of technical projects is exasperating; as Dr. Raley would say, I am completely devoid of any sensitivity to the most elemental principles of physics. . . .

To unscrew a jar lid, for instance, to refill the desk stapler or to attach the garden hose when the faucet is practically under the house and behind the shrubbery . . . figure that out. Locks, all locks, distress me. Keys seldom work, and sometimes I lose them. To hang a picture, replace a high lightbulb, to light the pilot, to close the fireplace damper, and oh, to check the circuit breaker—

these can be real crises. As to lifting my heavy suitcase into the trunk of the car, closing the vents in the attic, checking the reset on the TV . . . what's a woman to do?

And yet I *have* learned to live alone and to take care of myself. Through all the reordering of my life, there has come some serenity—a sort of reward for trying. I have nearly always been frightened, but I have learned to cope. The biggest problem has been that state of ambivalence, that daily battle between defeat and determination. A step forward, two backward—it has been a strange cadence.

There came a turning.

During part of a snowbound winter, I reread some Tolstoy. In the very last paragraph of *Anna Karenina*, the character, Levin, expresses what was supposedly Tolstoy's own experience: "Faith, or not faith. I don't know what it is, but this feeling has come perceptibly through suffering and has taken firm root in my soul . . ."

For me, the direction came from that vital, decisive, energetic "presence" who had taught me, through all the years we were together, something of his resilient faith toward guidance and dependence on a loving, concerned God whom we know and believe through his Son. I could no longer strive by myself, on my own. I had to have help, perspective, and an awareness of a life pattern that works toward eventual good.

My pain was lessened; I looked up for hope and motivation.

In my efforts to devise a workable thought pattern, I decided that some kind of happiness was to come from within my own being; paradoxically, it would also come through relationships outside myself. As Dr. James Angell writes in his wonderful little book, *Yes Is a World:*

You can't unring a bell,
You can't unshine a star,
You can't retrieve a word you've said—
The things that are, just are.

But you can accept the truth,
You can breathe deep and free,
You can, out of emptiness, create
A fact, and a flame, called Me. *

I looked to the examples of other women who have had to face (as we all have to face at times) binding circumstances, and who have accepted the challenge to rise above them. Maya Angelou, an interesting and profound thinker, has to her credit the long road from the Arkansas cotton fields to an impressive role in contemporary literature—a journey she has faced with compassion, humor, and style. Pearl Buck, who was never daunted by age or circumstances, said on her eightieth birthday, "I am a far more valuable person than I was fifty years ago."

Ann, the too-young widow of a university professor, was left with two small sons to support. While sorrow was new and close to the top, it became imperative that Ann make immediate plans to support herself and the boys. With no capital except her ingenuity and craftsmanship, this young mother turned an unfurnished room into kindergarten facilities. Now, after almost thirty years, the well-established and accredited school is still operating with several assistants under Ann's supervision. Her sons, professionally established now, and her other "children"— hundreds of them—have shared the courage which sur-

*James W. Angell, *Yes Is a World*, copyright © 1974, p. 85; used by permission of WORD BOOKS, PUBLISHER, Waco, Texas 76703.

faced through sorrow. Her involvement, outside herself but grounded by her personal faith, has become a saga of contentment and contribution to life about her.

Such inspiration is near all of us. The common denominator is need. Learning to live above grief is hard. Circumstances are never right; timing is off; the will is weak; things are imperfect. Living again, starting a new life, is a learning process. And there are rules:

1. Learn to accept and to use solitude; it has advantages—for restoring the soul, for cultivating "one's own garden."

2. Learn to use the resources I have . . . skills, education, money, physical assets, personality, position.

3. Learn to accept the "set apartness" of being a widow (although there are millions like us) as a fact of life.

4. Learn to stand on my own feet, get myself places under my own power, if at all possible.

5. Learn to handle my business with the best knowledge I have.

6. Learn to make decisions—some right, some wrong.

7. Learn to lay out the "next project" before finishing the present one.

8. Learn to color my days with cheer, hope, and love.

9. Learn to be grateful, to reach out, but not to depend on friends' good intentions.

10. Learn to make my own happiness; to be "a merry heart" if it kills me!

11. Learn and relearn what faith can do.

* * *

In learning to accept and adjust to my own widowhood, I have found a workable formula—one that is simple and worthy: every woman, striving toward a fulfilling life, needs a work to do, someone to love, and a God to believe in.

I shall hold on to that, step by step, day by day.

IV

Leftovers

"And when she got there, the cupboard was bare."

NURSERY RHYME

TIME TO START . . . "and when she got there, the cupboard was bare," or so it seemed after my husband died. My entire life seemed empty: I felt acutely my vulnerability and inadequacy. But it is amazing, I found, what one can do with a few leftovers. Sooner or later, everybody has to manage. There are assets and, if one looks for them, valuable resources.

I first learned about leftovers from a special friend. Eightyish, a tiny Dresden-doll woman, she is the widow of a renowned minister, one whom Baptists call "a great Christian statesman." I see her now . . . fluffy little curls, downy white, around a porcelain-textured face, the blue eyes bright with alertness. Pastels and violets, dainty little shoes and handbags, wispy face veils on once-stylish toques, and always gloves. This is my little friend. Knowledgeable and current, though just a little frightened of today's world, she is gallant in her widowhood. It is to her that I send my laciest, dreamiest, hearts-and-flowers pink valentine!

Across the miles, she writes to me. Arthritic little hands

peck out her miniature typewritten letters—little doll notes. These bespeak a chuckling sense of humor as well as a subtle insight, and at times contain sly thrusts at "the brethren," those pompous ones of the clergy who "with wrinkled brow and briefcase" occasionally call.

Her last note said, about retirement, "It is great to keep busy at worthwhile things, without having to search for them. How any retirees can be bored, I can't see, with opportunities camping on doorsteps to be stumbled over. They must like to stare at TV."

With no children, no family, surely her cupboard should be bare. On the contrary, for all her fragility, what delectable leftovers she uses for living. Take the memories, for instance—young romance that never grows old, friendships from pastoral days of scheduled activities. Tearoom luncheons with young friends, though more infrequent now, require a nod to up-to-the-minute fashions. Her husband's published works, the reading and the rereading . . . and a note to me, "How did he ever find the time?" The books—how she revels in them—the classics, the poetry of happier times.

There are, of course, good days and bad days. There is pain. There is aloneness in her own little world of high-rise apartment living. But the shelves are well stocked. Like the exquisite pieces of china that once enhanced the years of hostessing in the manse, precious and joyous bits of living fill her cupboard. And whatever is left over is put to use, perhaps on some fine spring day when there are violets. . . .

As I began to look and to plan, to think of options, to dream a little, I began to find leftovers I could use to build my new life. With university facilities nearby, there was opportunity to enroll for another degree, or to take courses in some special interest, or perhaps to just audit some classes. I was not interested. There were too many associations, too many memories everywhere I turned, and I was uncomfortable with the many changes that had taken place. I found it almost impossible to be objective.

It was the Chapel organ and a compelling desire to play such an instrument that inspired me to begin something new. Organ lessons, though intermittent, a few each semester, gave me confidence and some proficiency in performance, in reaching certain goals I set for myself.

Daily practice demanded a discipline I never thought I could muster. Alone, there in that tremendous auditorium, I would try to prepare my assignments, but from the great vaulted heights I kept hearing the magnificent resonance of the funeral music. So often, not even taking the time to change my organ shoes, I rushed home to cry, only to try again the next day.

There was encouragement from family and friends, and from grandchildren who were dutifully impressed. Best of all was the feeling of achievement in the cultivation of a resource I had never taken seriously. This leftover in the cupboard of my life can never be taken from me. And now, whenever glorious music swells and soars toward the Chapel spire, from the softest whispers of love to the greatest themes of triumph, I feel a strengthening and a gladness. I am about the business of living and of stretching toward my best.

The expansive Medical Center is adjacent to the university campus and just two fences beyond the "little" President's home. The building of this project was an absorbing interest in Dr. Raley's last years. Serving on the

Building Authority, he was as enthusiastic and vigilant about its construction as in those years of university building. Daily he checked on the progress, an incongruously familiar figure with his hard hat and his cane.

Because of his interest, I became involved in the Volunteer Women's Group, the Pink Ladies, if you please. We could not know, he and I, that so soon after the ribbon-cutting and all the formalities of dedication he would become one of the first patients. Room 210 overlooks our house. It is still hard for me to respond to calls from the second floor, and especially to deliver flowers and mail to 210, but the rewards are soul-satisfying. Somehow I feel needed.

If there are moments of depression or sadness in my volunteer work, they come as I try to respond to the needs of those women, many about my age, there in the hospital or in the adjacent convalescent home, who are utterly, completely alone in the world. This segment of our society increases in distressing proportions. Perhaps the last of the family, with no one to care where they are nor how they are, they become nameless, identified only by their room numbers. Abandoned, with little hope of gathering up life again, their leftovers are all used up, their cupboards are bare.

One tries to help, only to be thwarted by the complications of involvement, to say nothing of legalities, red-tape technicalities, and government regulations. But once in a while something will brighten the face of dejection and despair. Just a little something—a flower, a letter, maybe just a pat on a thin shoulder, or a "good morning!" One never forgets the moment; it works both ways.

Volunteer work at the hospital is its own reward. I

recommend it as therapy for sorrow and loneliness. It is now a part of my life.

Another resource I have found, untapped since my first year of college, is my class of private piano students whom I teach two afternoons a week. These are special days. A sense of accomplishment, of time well used, of contribution to the lives of the children and their families—these are the dividends far beyond reckoning. What some would call "tying yourself down to a schedule" is setting aside a block of time for something that is very important to me. Even when scales and exercises run through my head most of the night, or when I worry about those who won't practice, I am challenged by the thought that eventually there will be music. And I derive a selfish benefit from all those scales and exercises: as I play along, I keep up my technique. Perhaps tomorrow I shall play a little Chopin. Next week, I'll rework some Liszt, or make myself start something new.

Resources of time and love are provided by friends, those special people to whom an occasional note or contact makes all the difference in the day. I have found that keeping in touch is important, and although the expenditure of one's self takes some toll of energy, there is, in return, the reward of reaching out to others.

And cheers for television—good, bad, very bad, and innocuous! Only the most closed, reactionary mind would discount the benefits of this modern miracle, this widening dimension that opens up the world at the touch of a switch. From the most desolate adobe desert home to the sophistication of condominium living, the world is there!

For many women who live alone, television is the companionship, the voice, the contact with the world that makes the days bearable. Even the afternoon involvement in heart-rending soap operas has a point. It affords something beyond four walls.

Daytime watching is not on my list, but the evening curtain opens on Vienna and Strauss, opera at the Met, summer music from Boston Pops, the theater in London, Broadway musicals (give me an old, good movie any night in the week!), symphonies, concerts, great extravaganzas the world over. From household hints and medical advice (commercials notwithstanding) to classical literature and, of course, the Washington scene—all is available by touch. How fortunate we are to have such a resource, this private view of the world and the people in it.

Perhaps no leftover in these alone years has been more vitally replenishing and restorative than my old habit of reading. At long last, there is time to read all I want to, these evenings of mine when television has no appeal. It is an invaluable conditioning.

"One for the head and one for the heart"—that's what I have always said to the librarians at our Carnegie Library when I check out books. Long ago, as a very young college president's wife, I felt the need to improve my mind, to be knowledgeable and conversant on scholarly issues. Erudition became a primary discipline . . . that's why I said, "one for the head, please."

On the other hand, I am a born romantic, and all but addicted to the world of fiction and fantasy. Many a long, lonely evening becomes a delight when transported into realms of make-believe. Surely, psychology explains and commends such therapy.

Since I have been widowed, I've had more time and inclination for devotional reading: stacks of inspirational

volumes rest always on my nightstand, many of them
practically memorized. Some are of older vintage—*From
Sunset to Dawn* by Leslie R. Smith, Dr. Leslie D.
Weatherhead's *Will of God*, the C. S. Lewis books, particularly *A Grief Observed*, and Norman Vincent Peale's
Thought Conditioners and Spirit Lifters, which I have carried
in my purse the world over.

In Tileston's *Devotionals*, which I have read every
morning for two or three years, I noticed that certain days
seemed to have significant reading for me. On Dr. Raley's
birthday, I found his favorite scripture, "For God hath not
given us the spirit of fear; but of power, and of love, and of
a sound mind [translated 'discipline']" (2 Tim. 1:7). And on
the day of his death, this seemed appropriate: "And thus,
the man died, leaving his faith for an example of noble
courage and a memorial of virtue, not only to young men,
but unto all his nation . . ."

Yes Is a World, by Dr. James W. Angell, contains
contemporary thought I have needed, while Eileen Guder's
The Many Faces of Friendship related me to the world of
people again. *Grief's Slow Wisdom*, Cort Flynt's beautiful
little book of condolence, was as restoring as the visit I had
had with him when we were younger.

For woman-to-woman reading, no writer in our time is
more comforting than the gifted Catherine Marshall,
whose first husband, Peter, was the legendary Scottish
chaplain of the United States Senate in the late 1940s.
During that turbulent time in our history, and particularly
during the war years, Peter Marshall's prayers sustained
and heartened those powerful men in Washington, his
rolled *R*s and pithy phrases echoing through the halls of
Congress.

Those were not far-flung, high-sounding words; rather,

they were pragmatically thought, directly intoned, simply spoken. Each prayer was an eloquent call to faith and fortitude: "Stop us, O God, for a minute of prayer." "When we are overwhelmed by our sense of littleness in the world, may we remember that thou hast made us all different, hast given to each of us a purpose, and if we fail, it will never be fulfilled." "We know that our Christianity is no insurance policy against trouble, but rather the guarantee that thou wilt be with us in trouble. That should give us strong hearts and confident faith."

Each prayer reflected Peter Marshall's love for his adopted country. And because of Catherine, his prayers, beautifully edited, are to be shared in little booklets and greeting cards at every Hallmark Cards counter.

I met Catherine Marshall only once, a few years after her husband's death. I shall never forget our conversation, nor the subsequent exchange of letters and books. We had mutual friends who, long before I ever met her, had told me of their student days at Agnes Scott College and of the romance between Catherine and the dashing young Presbyterian minister in Atlanta. The movie version of their life together has become one of the box-office classics of all time.

Peter's death at age forty-six was mourned not only by official Washington and by all those blessed by his ministry, but also by the millions who have read Catherine's writings about him. Among the nationally known ranks of Christian stalwarts, there was an empty place, yet he himself had said, "The measure of a life, after all, is not its duration, but its donation."

It is through this experience that Catherine Marshall has comforted all of us.

One day I went to our local library to look through all

her books. Carefully, I handled the readable but worn-out copy of *A Man Called Peter*, the ragged pages barely held together by the binding. It was probably one of the most read books in the library. *Beyond Ourselves* was also well worn, and in places delicately underlined where some reader had stopped to think awhile. Like other widows, I lived through every page of *To Live Again*, her remarkable and inspiring account of her great sorrow, her adjustment and acceptance, her application of faith.

Somewhere, she wrote, "After Peter became my husband, he continued to mold me . . . not often is there such a combination of husband and teacher." Mine was a similar experience. Several years younger than Dr. Raley, helplessly inadequate, I felt, to share his ministerial career, I too was challenged by his patient coaching, his gentle guidance, his bearing, and, most of all, his indomitable faith. Even now, I ache to hear him preach, to feel the vibrancy of his unconquerable spirit.

Mrs. Marshall must have had the same feeling about Dr. Marshall's immortality. "Surely, there is a difference (and it is not just a quibble) between God's ideal will and His permissive will. Thus, in my case, I cannot believe that it was God's will that Peter Marshall die at forty-six. But, given a set of circumstances among them Peter's inherited physique, so fine that he was inclined to overtax it, God had an alternate plan by which He could bring unimagined good out of early death."

I must believe that, too—eventual good, a purpose, a reason to live.

Recently, I rechecked the underlying philosophy of *Beyond Ourselves*. So simply written, so richly lived, it is directed to all of us making our way in "rivers of difficulty," times of adjustment and acceptance. One finds answers—that life is accumulative, that we come into responsible maturity by and through relationships that touch our lives. "Each beloved person's place is his own for this life and eternity . . . no one can take it from him, nor does it impinge on anyone else's place. . . ."

Early in my widowhood, I felt destitute of spirit, emotionally empty. I was not able to counter the sense of incompleteness, nor could I ignore the compulsion to finish my husband's life. Many observed that he had died too young, that his stature was needed in the turbulence of a changing world, and particularly that of the university community.

I was the one who knew, better than anyone else, that he had lived his life up fiercely, intensely, in a selfless dedication. My concern was to gather up the bits and pieces of busy years, put them all together in an ordered profile of the man. At the same time, I began to think toward life without him and a revitalization of my own potential.

Over and over, I said the words, "In His will, there is peace." . . . "No purpose of Thine can be restrained." And in the effort toward some kind of order, some meaning to life, I decided that action just might be the most effective form of prayer. To the rhythm of the tires as I drove to visit John and Helen and their families; to the routine of keeping the house and yard, I began some restitution of being. To the discipline of thinking "one" instead of "two," achieving some degree of adjustment, only at times to regress into complete unacceptance, I began to face up to my grief, and gradually began to feel a sense of self. Unbelievably, there was a therapy in small goals, a cadence to the days.

The cupboard was not bare, then. Life can and does go

on. The residue of love is there to thrive, to ennoble. A friend, upon the death of her husband, a distinguished man of letters, wrote to me, "In each of us there is still a part of his undying spirit." I am thinking now that, although one adjusts and accepts, perhaps the chapter is never really closed. It's just that another begins. I have begun to understand that there is an immortality on earth, and that "though much is taken, much abides."

V

"The First Thing You Must Do Is Take a Cruise"

"Beauty without one's beloved is like a sword through the heart."

ROSETTI

I DIDN'T WANT TO GO on a cruise, but I did.

"Dr. Raley would not approve of your grieving this way," I was admonished. "You must go away for a while. Why not take a cruise? Now that's the thing to do. Or move into an apartment . . . get rid of this house and everything in it. Why not get a job? Or what would you think of going for a Master's?"

I listened without hearing. It was miserable, and it went on day after day.

There were such verbal thrusts as "You're a lot better off than most women," "Get hold of yourself," and "You simply cannot spend the rest of your life like this, and alone. . . ."

Everybody meant well, but every time I heard "Time will heal," I flinched involuntarily.

"The arrangements are absolutely perfect," I was told, "and this is the perfect time for you to get away."

I had no heart to counter the plans made for me. And so . . .

The luxury French cruise ship had docked at Ville-France after ten lazy October days of sailing turquoise seas through the Greek Islands and the Italian Riviera. Now occasional glimpses of pastel villas along the Mediterranean shore confirmed the end of the cruise. From the International Airport at Nice, the passengers would jet to New York. I sat on deck, musing over the trip and the life to which I would return.

Of the three hundred passengers on the ship's roster, eighty-six were widows—all types, all ages, all sizes. Usually in pairs—best friends, relatives, coworkers, or maybe old college roommates, they were easily identified as singles, women without men. There was a certain look about them, about us—of discard, of misfit, of sitting on the sidelines waiting. No matter how charming, how delightful, how beautifully groomed, we were marked women—not necessarily to be shunned, but to be detached from, if possible. It's the same on every tour—a phalanx of alone women seems to swarm onto ships, into buses, onto planes, and always to take advantage of rest stops.

On deck, in the lounge, everywhere, we compared notes: "We had done everything together. . . . When you marry, you do become one. Now I feel like half of my life, even more, is gone." "I didn't want to live, nor did I want to try to make another life for myself. It was too late to start over." "My greatest fear was being totally alone, having no one to really care for me, no one to live for." Or, "I was either too young or too old, I don't know which, to start living again."

Our society is not geared for singles, certainly not for widows. Everything happens two by two; it is a couple's world. And yet women who are alone are becoming an increasingly significant segment of the population. The statistics are mind boggling. Thirty percent of the adult women in the United States are widowed, separated or divorced, or have never married. One woman in six over the age of twenty-one is a widow. This "alone" group represents about 40 percent of the women's work force in the nation (statistics given are for 1977).

Each is an individual case, deeply personal, different from the next. Yet, when all cases are taken together, the "woman alone" syndrome takes on increasing portent. There are many ramifications—economics and health care, social and living patterns, spiritual and ethical values.

That is not to say the problems faced by widows are new. The ancient sage of faith, Job, was known as the champion of the wronged and the helpless: "I caused the widow's heart to sing for joy" (29:13), while Psalm 146:9 provides this comfort: "He relieveth the fatherless and the widow: but the way of the wicked he turneth upside down." Isaiah speaks out: "Plead for the widow," and Paul says, "Honour widows that are widows indeed" (2 Tim. 5:3).

Everybody knows the story about the widow's mite, inspired by the one who needed every penny to make ends meet. This the plight of the fixed-income widow caught in the grip of today's economic crisis.

Luke 18:5 gives a refreshing change in the widow image. In his parable of the unjust judge, Christ not only taught persistence in prayer but commended the stance of justified wrath against wrong: "Yet because this widow troubleth me, I will avenge her, lest by her continual coming she weary me"—a salute, if I ever heard one, for all those women who crusade for a better world.

It is true that today's woman is often better prepared for widowhood than she once was. With due respect to the concepts of women's liberation, she has a chance for developing identification and a sense of self-worth before she is widowed. Society in the last generation has created a climate for a woman to be both an independent spirit and a supportive wife and mother. Should widowhood come, she is a long way from the biblical connotation of deprivation and pathos—a pitiful, helpless creature to be defended from exploitation.

Devastation and collapse do not necessarily follow the death of a husband. In my case, it did. Because my husband was the one (I thought) indestructible factor of my whole existence, it never occurred to me that I would someday have to live without him. When a close friend, a minister's wife, had told me of her definite plans, if and when the time came, to take some volunteer post, preferably on a foreign mission assignment for her church, I had almost been repulsed by the idea. That was a long time ago; now, I wish I had made such plans, no matter how difficult the projection.

How, then, does one prepare for widowhood? How can a wife become objective enough to think past the phobia of inhibiting restraints, the widow image, and the fear of the unknown, to line up her options "just in case"? There is much advice to be found, from columns in the newspapers to medical journals, from religious "encounter" groups to hobby crafts. There is a decided advantage to working outside the home; working women learn to face the world every morning, no matter what circumstances prevail.

The last two decades have produced a wide range of reading most helpful to any woman who must cope with the almost certain eventualities of life alone. In her book, *A Life of Your Own*, Harriet La Barre writes, "Be true to yourself, honest about who you are and what you want out of life, worrying very little, if at all, about what 'they' think." Easier said than done, but I like that. Although such an attitude requires an extra measure of determination and courage and a lot of bravado, it just may work.

Hobbies and interests can form the basis for a fulfilling widowhood. A professor's widow went back to teaching to support herself and her two high-school-aged children. But after managing to send them to college, she began to think about herself. A latent interest in drama suggested a respite from the eight walls of home and classroom. She decided to join a community theater staff as a wardrobe helper. Soon her costume creations, authenticated by research, became works of art. Talent and skill began to pay off, and more opportunities came her way. New interests gave her a new look. Today she is a sought-after designer in the theater.

And then there's Dotty, a forever-friend in the business world who will never get around to all her hobbies. For many years she has maintained herself, lives well, and has never been daunted by misfortune, bad luck, or what people think.

Dotty goes on hobby-binges. They last a year or two, and then she thinks up another. I first knew her when women all wore hats, never appearing on the street or in public without the right one. Dotty's specialty at that time was the creation of such good-looking, stylish hats that we all beat a path to her door. Soon she was making our purses to match. Finest tailoring projects followed; her family was always well dressed.

And then there was the gardening era, the music era (reviving a long-forgotten talent). Oil painting lasted through satisfying years. Years of canning and preserving were followed by stints at photography and jewelry-making. Always there was the wonderful feeling that life was good, interesting and exciting, and that one mustn't miss a minute.

Few march to such a drummer, but there is a point in developing whatever talents and interests one has.

Looking ahead toward widowhood can help ease the passage into the new life alone. Yet no matter what preparation is made, one is never quite prepared for the emotional impact of being suddenly unattached. No longer is it anybody's responsibility to keep the widow occupied, surrounded by solicitude, assured of constant vigilance. The "widow woman" is on her own. Sometimes even one's children cannot understand; they equate freedom, time, reasonable security and health with contentment and an easy life. "Do what you want to, Mother" is meant to be reassuring.

And so, widows cling together—at the country club, at the theater. They sit together at church; they pick each other up for meetings or for shopping jaunts, for crafts classes, for work. Stoically, many women continue to hold on to their jobs, no matter how trying or unremunerative, just to keep contact with people. Others wait for dutiful visits from family and friends, while a resigned boredom begins to show in both mental and physical problems.

Even today, evenings are very difficult for me. A woman does not go out unescorted. She is warned of the danger in driving alone, of coming into her home without some protection. To impose on friends, especially couples, for transportation is usually unsatisfactory, and often inconvenient. As much as I enjoy entertaining, it aways hurts just a little. The awful emptiness is there, no matter how many people fill the rooms. And so my days are kept full, but the evenings linger.

Loneliness, "the awful predicament of mankind," as Taylor Caldwell refers to it, is a painful problem for a widow. On the women's page of a daily newspaper, the headline, "Loneliness Can Kill You," grabbed my attention. The article was about the preventive medicine of companionship, the importance of family life and caring for friends and neighbors. It included a survey report that single, widowed, and divorced people are more likely prey to disease than are married people. In the same article, a physician was quoted as saying that failure to form human relationships imperils both life and health, and that basic unhappiness accounts for 50 percent of all illness.

And so, we die of loneliness and lovelessness, the need to love and be loved. In 1936, for the whole world to hear, King Edward VIII, the Duke of Windsor, stated his case: "Loneliness is not simply a matter of being alone; loneliness is that feeling that nobody else truly cares what happens to you."

Why is loneliness such a pervasive sickness in our society? An article on loneliness in the September 1976 issue of *Our Times*, the splendid publication of the Seventh Day adventist denomination, suggests that our industrial society and the mobility of the population has brought about a feeling of impermanence, that millions feel lost in anonymity.

The pressure of the times also accounts for much loneliness. With the increase in population, there is a trend toward withdrawal. Consumed by their own interests, people generally are unwilling to pay the price of involvement, or in some cases, to risk danger or fraud. Nobody is more aware of this than the lonely widow, who may be at the mercy of well-intentioned friends, or even of children busy with their own lives. "A man that hath friends must shew himself friendly" (Prov. 18:24), is applicable and workable, though discretion is, in these times, advisable.

Another contributor to loneliness, especially for women, is the lack of self-esteem. Feelings of inferiority can constrict personality and devalue constructive qualities, resulting in further isolation. It's a vicious cycle; loneliness begets more loneliness.

Therapists persuade us that the solution for loneliness is not to be found in escape or excitement or entertainment, but within one's self and in relationships with others. Service, they contend, is a healing force; the joy of being a part of something bigger, better, and more enduring than self is an antidote to loneliness. Reaching out is essential.

In their book, *Master Your Tensions and Start Living Again*, George Stevenson and Harry Milt set me straight: "Remember other people are busy working out their social arrangements and taking care of their own affairs. They don't have the time and interest to seek you out, and to involve you in their activities if you've taken yourself out of circulation. They assume that you just don't care to be bothered, or else they forget about you entirely as you drop out of the forefront of their attention."

In later years it is not easy to reach out, to re-create and to redirect one's life. It requires making the best of a situation until a better way is found, being alert to every advantage. In Philippians 4:11, Paul suggests a well-being that heartens me: "I have learned, in whatsoever state I am, therewith to be content." Another verse, 4:13 is helpful: "I can do all things through Christ, who strengtheneth me."

I dared to open up this idea on the ship one day when a group of us sat in deck chairs, basking in beautiful weather along the serene shores. "Self-assurance," I suggested, "is what we all need, or perhaps the word is self-esteem. It could become real, you know." And I thought of Eliza in the Pygmalion fantasy, *My Fair Lady,* longingly singing, "Wouldn't it be loverly?"

Later, in my stateroom, I wrote down a few guidelines for myself—a practical exercise. There was no magic involved in these simple goals, but they pointed the way toward beginning to feel a part of the world in which I struggled to live. They pointed the way to a life that would be less lonely . . .

I am a responsible adult woman. I know who I am and where I am going. . . . I will be smart enough to know where I stand—financially, physically, emotionally. I can think of something better ahead. The Oral Roberts line has merit: "Something good is going to happen to you." It is a matter of planning to live better, more comfortably, even managing a little touch of luxury once in a while (I deserve it). . . . Once a hostess, always a hostess. Entertaining will be very simple—a few friends occasionally, a couple for supper, a neighbor for a cup of tea, a small luncheon, a little holiday party at home. . . . It is important to keep the telephone ringing, to maintain interest in a variety of things, even if I have to bluff it. Most of all, I need to try to find somebody to talk to, a good conversationalist who will keep me updated on current affairs. . . . I shall protect my precious time, saving some for my own blessedness; I must remember that body care, clothes care, good grooming, etc. take time, lots of it. . . . Let me look forward to something special every day, no matter how trivial, and make plans in advance. Though living in a world of casual convenience, my little retired friend has never given up the satisfaction of being beautifully dressed and coiffured for her dinner—the linen place mat, the fragile china, the sparkling silver and crystal . . . and recorded music. . . . I'm going to try for one trip a year—a short one will do—just for a change of pace and scene. I am going to keep a calendar and fill in all the blanks. Most of all, I am going to try to be a more caring person; they say it works both ways. . . . And yes—I will try to pick, or at least smell, some daisies once in a while.

A brave front for the world out there! On the cruise ship, I touched base with a new hope for living with the aloneness of widowhood.

I was disconcerted, however, to discover that loneliness came home with me. The therapy was stymied. My new life, all those plans and projects, didn't always work. Like everybody else who loses heart occasionally, I had to learn what I was supposed to know—that only the cultivation of a divine Presence could assuage my distress and doubt, that only this Constancy would prevail through recurring efforts to rebuild my life, to restore my faith. "Behold, I stand at the door" changed my thinking. Remembering, over and over, to open that door helped keep me going.

One morning after my return from the cruise I set out to do all those catch-up errands that crash one back into the reality of routine.

It was a lovely day. Following rain, a lush green shimmered over our town. Everything was in bloom. My attention was projected upward, outward, over—a sort of exultation. As Thoreau had written, there in his beautiful world of Walden, one cannot be melancholy in the midst of such beauty. Such abounding loveliness in nature was an assurance of immortality. I had felt while on the ship that surely life goes on . . . somewhere. I had the same feeling on this new day, here in the peaceful realms of home—that I was to be sustained, even in those lonely-heart places where no one could enter.

At the door of the gift shop, not yet opened, I met Kay, whom I had not seen recently. She too had been on a cruise. We laughed about being early risers, about being up and out and on our way.

Kay and I had been widowed about the same time, after good and happy married lives. I asked, "How do you like living in an apartment? What was it like to leave your beautiful home where there were so many memories? It must have been quite an adjustment."

Kay answered positively. It had been the only thing to do: she had all the room she needed, was free of yard maintenance, and was close enough to her children without interfering in their lives. All the right reasons, and pure logic, I thought.

Then we talked about travel, the places we had been, where we would like to go. . . . "There are so many of us, Kay. We all lost our husbands about the same time in our lives—this is almost a widow's town. Do you ever get lonely? And can you leave your loneliness at home when you go on trips?" I told her that I couldn't—not yet.

"Oh, that's the way it is," she agreed. "Sure, I get lonely, but I'm learning to live with it. I go to the kitchen and cook, invite somebody over for dinner and a visit. . . ."

The gift shop opened. We decided to get together more often, and perhaps go on a trip together.

The day stretched ahead. I began to check off errands.

On the way home, I said a little prayer for courage to extend myself toward something or somebody, for energy and spirit to rechannel my life into significance, and—most of all—for strength to pay the price for not being lonely.

The bruises of loss are beginning to fade. The sword could go no deeper. And remembered beauty of time and place and love transcends the loneliness.

From here to there, over the horizon, the vistas are bright.

VI

An Unfinished Chapter

"The Lord will perfect that which concerneth me."

PSALM 138:8

SUMMER, 1974.

It was a superhuman project.

As somebody said, the floor was strewn with memories. Literally, it was covered with stacks of filing cases— twenty-five or thirty, as I recall, bulging with presidential papers, correspondence, public statements, publications, scrapbooks, photographs, recordings, and tapes. Thirty-five years of administrative tenure at the university, one man's life, was now to go into cardboard boxes.

Since Dr. Raley's death, I had felt an increasing responsibility to organize this voluminous material into a collection to be housed permanently in the west wing of the John Wesley Raley Chapel. Now I had dedicated the summer to the task of sorting and cataloguing.

The hours spent in the library of our home that sweltering summer were incalculable; the days strung together in an exhausting, all-consuming pattern. The necessary sorting of memorabilia brought back all the memories of the sorrow that had so changed my life—some clear in focus, haunting and hurting, some fading into the blessedness of a miracle.

Then finally, the work was finished. Sixteen years after the dedication of the Chapel, alumni, faculty, and friends joined our family for the presentation of a collection that reflected considerably more than half the life of the university. Looking around the room—the bright red file boxes lining one wall, the fireplace designed from leftover pieces of marble from the Chapel, the antique glass-fronted cabinet that had once been a bulletin board and was now the repository for Dr. Raley's academic regalia—I was aware that a chapter in our lives had been completed. I could forget the long, grueling days of reading and sorting, the isolation, the forcing of my mind to remember everything . . . It was time to start something new.

For six years, I had tried to believe that God worked toward good in each faltering effort, not only in the completion of this historical chapter, but also in the rebuilding of my own life. Still so bereft, I often had to hold my head up high to keep the tears from falling—a stance mistaken sometimes for loftiness. Now I felt a longing toward some challenge of service, the need to stretch toward some goal, perhaps to find a job for which I might be qualified.

What could I do? What could I do best? What did I have to work with? Did I have enough faith in God's concern for a personal need like mine? Would the ultimate good work out if I were just willing to try? Could I become unselfconscious, objective? To find the answers, one stares at nighttime ceilings, puts out a hand only to touch an empty space, and prays for help, for release.

When the telephone rang at six o'clock one dark winter morning, I knew it was my recently widowed friend and confidante, a retired career teacher. She too was trying to adjust to the loss of her husband, a prominent banker who had died after a long and tragic debilitation.

"I've been awake so long. Can you listen?" Mary Ann asked.

"Yes, I need to hear a voice, too. It's so quiet. Did you know it snowed last night?" I answered quickly.

"Well, I've just read something . . . 'In the day when I cried [and I can't seem to quit] thou answeredst me, and strengthenedst me with strength in my soul.' That's in Psalm 138, I think. Now, listen to this: 'The Lord will perfect that which concerneth me.' Now what do you think? Does that mean us?"

"Oh, I hope so, Mary Ann," I answered.

"Now, Helen, listen—I am convinced this is for us," she answered brightly. "Let's put our minds to it. I think it will work. Let's try!" Her sparkling faith came through, inspiring me.

"All right!" I countered. "With a lot on my mind this morning, most of it just indecision about a lot of things, I read this somewhere—'Action is the highest form of prayer.'"

We decided to get going, and to report to each other later; we both felt that something new would surely work out for us.

After hanging up, I went to sit at Dr. Raley's desk in our home. Mornings at his desk had become a sort of grounding for the day. Sitting in the familiar chair with the two-inch rubber cushion (Dr. Raley was a short man), I would switch on the light in the dawn darkness; look at the calendar, and travel keepsakes, the children's pictures; turn pages . . . this was the routine.

Taking stock, while watching the snow whirl and drift, I

admitted to myself that some of the goals I had set for another year were probably just wishful thinking. Fleeting impressions of some design were shadowy and elusive, with little evidence of guidance. I still felt a desperate need for some outlet of expression. And all the while, little bits of precious time were being fretted away.

A calculating look at my situation revealed available assets: a disciplined bent of mind, an almost inflexible feeling about keeping a schedule, a sincere desire for a life with some meaning. And I felt a certain fulfillment and sense of well-being about writing—the proven therapy of a pencil in hand. As long as I could remember, I had wanted to write . . .

Methodically, as she did everything else, my mother had prepared me for my education. During my five-year-old summer, she started me on my letters. In her Spencerian handwriting, especially fancy on capitals, she would arrange the ABCs across the blue lines of a Big Chief tablet for me to copy over and over. At night, before he read the paper, Papa would have me copy his neat figures in even rows just like he did on the cotton accounts. He believed in sharp pencils. I would often have to wait patiently while he sharpened mine with the big knife he always carried in his pocket.

My big brother, Tim, also helped prepare me for school. Often he would bring his pencils and tablets home to me— sometimes storybooks, sometimes classics. Pretending to read, I would turn the pages of his Latin and algebra books, or the Greek mythologies. Holding the books right side up didn't matter until later; words were fascinating.

Sometimes I would copy them; sometimes, I would write family names.

In our town, everybody eventually had Mrs. Tippen for a teacher. Upon her retirement after forty-plus years of teaching, it was estimated that she had taught over half the permanent population in town—sometimes the third generation. She had taught Tim; soon, it was my turn.

A tyrant for good grammar, both spoken and written, Mrs. Tippen would drill us mercilessly on parts of speech, moods and tenses, conjugations, punctuation, and spelling. Appalled at the misuse of personal pronouns, she was simply stunned by split infinitives and dangling participles.

Mrs. Tippen said that knowledge of the classics was essential if one wanted to write or speak well. So up and down the aisles we read the classics, paragraph by paragraph. In her time, and in mine, there were no shortcuts to learning, no workbooks, no psychological tests nor aids, no blanks to fill out. True and false questions hadn't been thought of. Inescapably, we became literate.

With this background, freshman college English held no terrors for me. Miss Birdie, in her dainty, high-necked flowered voile and with a tiny bunch of violets atop her pearl-encrusted backhair comb, was an extension of Mrs. Tippen. She had dedicated her life to the education of young women and to the daily use of *Ball's Constructive English* text, from which we dared not depart. In all the expansive fantasies of college life, I knew that some day I would write all I wanted to, but I could not know then that this deep and satisfying resource would later become a healing for sorrow.

From my mother I learned to be a compulsive letter writer. As a little girl, I would sit with her on letter-writing afternoons, marveling at the magic words that told her mother and members of her family all about life on our farm and in town, her various projects, how the children were growing, the crops and the weather.

In the same way, when I was at college I introduced my mother and father to dormitory and campus life, to my teachers and friends, to my schedule. This habit later served me well; my days as the wife of a college president were often spent at my upstairs spinet desk writing invitations by the hundreds, congratulatory notes, condolence expressions, alumni newsletters, faculty and trustee greetings, and all such public relations efforts for university good will.

My first "professional" writing came years later, in the 1940s. A column I wrote for the student newspaper at OBU, "My Day," won prizes and later became the basis for books of university memoirs. Under Dr. Raley's encouragement, I began to write free-lance articles for various other publications.

It was on a modern missionary journey to the Orient in 1963 that I first saw the possibility of other forms of writing. What proved to be a turning point was a suggestion from my husband. As our plane lifted and we waved to our missionary hosts, who stood on the upper ramp of Kai Tak airport, Dr. Raley leaned across me for one more look at Hong Kong. Then he said, "You must write this story, the remarkable enterprise of modern missions. . . . Why don't you write about Dr. Beddoe?"

And so I began writing the biography of our friend Dr. Robert E. Beddoe, that dashing young Dallas, Texas, doctor who had gone to South China in 1910, spending forty years there as a medical missionary. Very little had ever been written about his career. How diligently I had to work through what little material was available—some newspaper clippings, a few personal letters, hospital reports, and family pictures. Long conversations with Mrs. Beddoe provided the most valuable information. The process of writing involved research into Chinese historical background and culture, and into the effect of two world wars.

Almost apologetically, I set up appointments with editors and publishers, Dr. Raley insisting all the time that I was to do this on my own. There was slight interest, but certainly no definite commitment.

Five years went by. In the meantime, my "book" was stacked in a cardboard box, the chapters written and rewritten several times. This was an extra in my life, for the university schedule never slackened. There was still some hope that the work might be published if I could ever find the time to polish the manuscript.

Both time and schedule stopped for me on that day in May, 1968, when Dr. Raley's heart would no longer sustain him through hopeless surgery. During the time of numbness, of decision-making, of trying to get my bearings, I gave no thought to the book I had started.

And then, one day, I found the box, the stacks of pages all clipped into chapters. Was there a chance, I wondered? I wrote Word Books in Waco, Texas, who had expressed a slight interest before. The reply was that the editors were interested, and that a new editor would soon join the staff. It was Mary Ruth Howes, the daughter of missionaries to China, who became my mentor. Within a few months,

Doctor in an Old World was published, its attractively designed Oriental cover a factor in the launching and selling.

I was never to doubt God's working toward good during that time, not only in the provision of an editor who was familiar with the background material, but also in the unusual success of the sales technique. Beyond my fondest dreams, I had become a writer. With contract and copyright intact, I was listed in all the right places as an author. Speaking engagements filled my calendar. Reviews were quite extravagant. An effective dramatization was performed in Dallas, Texas.

Even before *Doctor in an Old World* was on bookshelves, the editors asked whether I would write the story of Dr. Raley's life. Was it too soon, the grief still too close to the top? The advice of family and friends notwithstanding, I was soon off on another project and, exactly one year after writing "Chapter I" across a page, I saw the first finished copies of *An Uncommon Man*.

Through all the pain of writing Dr. Raley's life story, his words kept me going. "I believe if a man is willing to surrender his will to God, he can do anything he wants to with his life," he had said to a senior student who was discouraged about going to medical school. Now it was up to me to believe it, so I kept going.

To condense such a full and dramatic career, such a powerful and exuberant personality, into a prescribed number of pages was a formidable job. In eight months, I had read all the correspondence, had sorted through countless presidential files of documents and personal papers, sermon notes, and trustees' minutes. In addition, there were one hundred fifteen university scrapbooks to check, as well as specification and information on eighteen buildings.

But the very activity itself became evidence of guidance. Although every letter, every picture, clipping, and tape was fraught with painful memories, I was aware of encouragement. He lived again to help me, just as he had always done. In some mystical way, I was able to reach through some dimension to where he was—still strong, still vital. Then I could understand Thornton Wilder's phrase: "There is a land of the living and a land of the dead . . . and the bridge is love."

I had had such an intimation before, long ago, when we were together. It had been a fleeting perception—indefinable, unacknowledged, yet very real. How strange that I should remember it after all the years; perhaps the experience of grief "through a glass, darkly" in time makes things more clear.

In 1955 the world had been gradually recovering from World War II and Korea. While visiting Edinburgh, Scotland, we had climbed the hills that overlook the gray gloom of the city to the ancient Edinburgh Castle. The whole panorama had suggested to me an indomitable ruggedness that not only projected back in time but also reflected a stunning awareness of the present.

Brightly colored tartans and flags, as well as precisely designed flower beds of autumn brilliance, had colored the scene as Dr. Raley, Helen, and I approached the massive stones of the nearby Scottish War Memorial. In that silent, whispered world of heather and moors, of grandeur and fortitude, we had read the prophetic words from Isaiah

chiseled in the magnificent frieze: "But they that wait upon
the Lord shall renew their strength; they shall mount up
with wings as eagles. . . ."

I was to recall those words many times over the years,
often paradoxically in darkest hours. I had felt it that day
when the Chapel was draped in black. Now I felt it in the
reassuring response to *An Uncommon Man*. The letters,
reviews, and requests were stacked on my desk:

"When can you start another book?"

"I read all night, laughing all the time, then crying."

"How wonderful that God has brought this talent into
view, at a time when you need it most."

"I couldn't put the book down. . . . One wants to read it
without interruption."

"You have brought him alive for a nice visit."

"People who never knew him can know him now, just
by reading your book."

The editor wrote, "The finished copy has just come to
my desk. I am proud of you."

And from a stranger: "Tonight I began a book I bought
this afternoon. It is now almost morning. I have read all
night, so moved and fascinated by the story of this
'uncommon man' that I had to keep on reading."

A little triumph on my own, a measure of satisfaction
and perhaps some contribution to the memories of great
men—these intangibles accrued daily through my writing.
There was a sadness, too, a longing to share it all with the
one who loved me most and who had inspired the writing.

My next writing venture was the hardest of all. Because
of so many requests for Dr. Raley's writings, my next
project was to condense these into a little memorial volume

to be called *The Golden Days and the Gallant Hours.* The work was even more painful than the biography had been, more personal somehow. It required patient sorting through scribbled notes on scraps of paper, deciphering hurriedly scrawled outlines and sometimes trying to complete his thoughts. There was anguish in having to select so little out of so much, challenge in tightening, condensing, "listening" to his voice.

How lifeless the words seemed now, so bereft of color and personality. But I could remember the intonations, the gestures, the hush of dramatic pauses. I could see the word pictures, all those "purple passages" that took us up the stairways of heaven, the pink and gold mornings, the shimmering pastels of his sunsets. My task was to try to ensure that the riveting personality came through.

Finally it was finished, the elegant little book bound in maroon, touched with gold. It was time to turn to something else, something on my own.

When a part of one is gone, can the other part carry on? We had been a team, he and I, my own identity absorbed in him and his career. Now could I take up his life, his extraordinary spirit, with continuing spirit, with continuing purpose? Could I be his voice through the writing he had never had time to do? Could I try to finish the chapter we had started so long ago, or start a new one? Many women have, and with amazing fortitude. They too have "mount[ed] up with wings as eagles."

Sitting at the desk that winter morning, I realized that this—the writing—was the direction I needed to take. This was what he had planned for me—the implementation of the most apt resource I had. And it was, if I could keep on believing it, the working of God's promise toward good. It was new territory.

And so I began serious free-lance efforts. Some paid off. Fan mail was interesting and encouraging. Even in some exultation, however, about this daring new goal, I was aware of limitations and the haunting dread of failure. There were many down days. And there were countless rejection slips, but I kept at it, a discipline of several hours a morning.

"Get up and get away from that desk . . . forget it!" several close friends told me.

"You can write when you are an old, old lady," my daughter insisted.

"You are going to destroy yourself," was for a time a very real concern of someone I trusted.

Once I had to decide between a trip to Europe and finishing a book. I stayed home . . . and finished the book.

Over all the protests, I held my ground. I was finding some peace of mind, some contentment.

This was part of an unfinished chapter. It was the going on, the reaching out . . .

"Write something every day," the experts suggest to would-be writers. It was like the piano practice I had done all my life—daily and disciplined, and alone. As dismal as this sounds to me, the pattern worked, even in discouraging situations.

At last, life began to have some meaning. I could understand how Catherine Marshall felt about her own writing. She has said that creative power comes at the point of helplessness. Surely, then, a restructured life is possible although one has to fight fear and disappointment, and sometimes defeat. The compulsion to survive, however, is strong, if one can emerge into some expression, even the tedious process of putting words across the page, just one after another, to cross out, to start over.

"I can help you," I could hear Dr. Raley say. He was remembering that I always wanted to write. It was as though I went out to meet him. He was alive, vigorous, optimistic, looking ahead in his infinitude, and yet back over his shoulder in love and approval.

The chapter, our chapter, could be finished. And as opportunity began to unfold for me, a new chapter was beginning.

VII

A Certain Grace,
A Certain Glory

"If I have found grace in Thy sight, show me Thy glory."

I SAT AT MY DESK, a pencil in hand, my mind a blank.

At a time when the women's liberation movement was beginning to reach significant proportions in the midwest, I had been asked to speak to the Oklahoma Conference for Women. This annual three-day seminar on the campus of Oklahoma State University attracts a cross section of women from many fields of interest—from farm and ranch housewives to big-city business executives.

Most of the participants would be singles, widows—women alone like me. What could I say to these women with any degree of certitude? What would inspire their sense of selfhood, the survival of their spirit in today's world?

I was well aware that things were radically different now from what they had been in "my day." It was a new world, one in which much of what I thought important had been devalued. I had been unprepared for the decline of once-observed social mores, the malaise of the counterculture. To me, the world of casual behavior trends, fraught with rebellion and denigration, was abrasive and ugly. In trying to adjust to the collegiate madness of the sixties and early seventies, I felt overcome with frustration. Reading Alvin Toffler's *Future Shock*—every page of it—had been a haunting experience.

Disoriented, as though I had been on another planet, or recovering from a coma, I faced a world that seemed to have changed overnight. And I was a casualty of that change, not only in my personal life, but in my public image. The status quo had shifted, and I felt diminished by strangeness, embarrassed by helplessness in a society that to me seemed dissolute in its raucous causes, sleazy fashions, and perverted art forms.

It was with this background that I had accepted the invitation. Now I wondered what I would say. The program coordinator had requested that I address some topic relevant to the emerging role of women in what TV commentator Charles Collingwood has called "the discontinuous world," so I chose to speak on the power of women on the American scene.

Tentatively, I wrote across the top of the paper, "Unto you it is given a certain grace, a certain glory." Then, below it, I added, "In today's world, however, we must be totally realistic. . . ."

I smiled as I remembered what Caroline K. Simon, the former New York Secretary of State, had said in an address to the Association of Industrial Nurses—that there are four things every woman needs to know: how to look like a girl, how to act like a lady, how to think like a man, and how to work like a dog! Facetious, perhaps, but the idea made headlines, and it may well be today's imperative.

Partial preparation for my thinking at this time had been

reading Isbel Ross's *Power with Grace,* the biography of
Mrs. Woodrow Wilson. Mrs. Wilson's strange and sometimes misunderstood role in American history has no
parallel. Both before and after the President's death, her
intense devotion to his cause is one of the great sagas of the
twentieth century. In reading about her, I was aware of
her unfaltering spirit, her formidable stance that justified
the book's reference to Hemingway's line: "Courage is
power with grace."

The author condenses the book with this characteriza-
tion: "Time dimmed old animosities; she had outlived
waves of criticism and the buoyant spirit that carried her
through many crises left her at the end with a strong sense
of optimism and fulfillment. Her own accomplishments
were lost in the dramatic sweep of a revolutionary idea, but
she never thought of honors for herself. It was enough for
Edith Boling to be remembered only as the wife of
Woodrow Wilson. That, to her, was the greatest honor of
all."

In all history, we can probably count on our fingers the
women who have wielded the kind of power Mrs. Wilson
held; countless ones, however, under modest circumstances, have changed the course of human events with
their strength and idealism. There is grace and glory
inherent in being a woman. It is inescapable, although the
built-in power is unrecognized, as is that resourceful
courage that surfaces when demanded.

The status of women, an issue currently under debate,
may well determine the future of our country. The
momentum of this power pulses strongly today, and we are
all affected by it. Converging currents of social change
affirm feminism as an idea whose time has come, one that

is here, although hopefully with some modification, to stay. Its directives involve those three verbs: to have, to get, to go. This means more education, more expression in the arts, the humanities, and politics, more executive positions.

But while women are demanding and getting more control over their lives, they still want a workable formula, guidelines for a burgeoning world. Many women are apprehensive in today's world, helpless in the face of the encroaching problems of inflation, health care, even personal safety. The white-gloved charm, the traditional daisy chains and ivy, the beauty queens and collegiate proms, the traditional young-matron image, and many proprieties of acceptable grace are back in another world, another time. Once, instinctive femininity belied the paradox of fiber; now, it ponders the threatened dehumanization of personality, the destruction of the human spirit.

Lost in the maze of my thinking, I wanted hope for what lay ahead for all women. And I wanted faith to believe that it is in the realm of the spirit that women rise to their highest idealism, their divine difference.

Perhaps no one in our time symbolizes such strength and fortitude as well as Mrs. Joseph P. Kennedy, that gallant lady of Boston and Hyannisport. On every page of *Times to Remember* one is inspired by her faith, that power expressed in the John Buchan line, "I know not age, nor weariness, nor defeat." Her faith, she says, is the "most important element in life, putting everything in spiritual focus"—that determination makes the pain bearable. Surely, this is the key to the remarkable strength that has survived war deaths, tragic personal disappointments, and two brutal assassinations.

Another heroine of mine now past eighty and still going strong, is Adela Rogers St. Johns, outspoken and irrepressible journalist of the twenties and thirties, confidante of movie kings and queens and, of late, the author of that most provocative novel, *Tell No Man*. She believes that there is considerably less greatness among American women today than ever in our history. In her *Some Are Born Great*, a gallery of both sung and unsung women who changed lives around them, she writes, "so here are my women. I don't think any of them ever heard the word, 'liberated'; they knew naturally what they were, and that they could soar as high as they wanted to at any time." A partial list of her heroines includes Amelia Earhart, Rachel Carson, Anne Morrow Lindbergh, Bess Truman, Marie Dressler, and even lovable, gifted Judy Garland. Each in her own way contributed to the common good. Each gave of herself, and, in varying degrees, of her skill and intelligence, ability, endurance—all those qualities of influence.

There are no easy answers to the complexities which women, young and older, single and married, face in the next decades. Both external and internal forces contribute to the dilemma. But in today's world, as in the lives of these modern heroines, it is still women's business to make life better, to make tomorrow better than today.

It is easy for a widow to become more impressed with her own helplessness than with her capacity to improve the quality of life around her. Lonely, grieving, often faced with the necessity of supporting herself and perhaps her children, she feels anything but powerful and courageous. Striving to keep up appearances, to maintain her standards of personal dignity, a widow constantly fights the battle of futility. Well-meaning advice to live as normally as possible is all but worthless; it can't be done. There is little hope for remarriage, if the idea were even remotely thinkable. Unmarried women outnumber single men by 26 percent, and outnumber widowers five to one.

An area of widowhood rarely mentioned is a person's innate need for attention, affection, and even physical love. Few women deny this need. Even in this era of casual convenience and uninhibited social conduct, most women are bound by those virtues of convention and good breeding. Touched by any suggestion of concern or interest, a widow fears that the slightest response might be misjudged. She is naïvely vulnerable to kindness, and though flattered by attention, she sometimes grows hostile toward any advances.

For whom, her femininity, that grace and glory of her womanhood? "What's the use?" a widow insists, uncomfortable with her own self-effacement, her depleting feelings of unimportance.

A capable, matriarchal character in Helen Van Slyke's *The Place to Be* gives an answer: "I can't sit here, stagnating, accepting crumbs of friendship and dutiful expressions of respect. . . . That was a trap into which many women often fell, a prison built of timidity and inertia. It was like meekly waiting for death. Life isn't coming to me at my age. I've got to go out and find it, at least fight boredom with some kind of action. . . ." She had no idea what she would do, but the doing was the important thing.

Sitting there at my desk, staring at the paper, I recognized the picture. Although I had come a long way, I was still looking for something. After nine years, my need

was even more acute. A dry, withering emotion had
become chronic.

Now, I wanted a gladness, a vitality, a sense of direction
I could share with the women at the conference. I wanted
to set my sails toward something worthy and perhaps
wondrous. C. S. Lewis had written about the secret
signature of the soul, the unappeasable want . . . and then,
"Here, at last, is the thing I was made for." That's what I
really needed.

I became aware that, for many reasons, it was necessary
to forget all negatives and, in the remustering of resources,
to begin to register the positive. I was ready to turn
another corner, to learn to make brick without straw if I
had to. As Anne Baxter said in her delightful book,
Intermission, "routine clicked its heels" and I was on my
way . . . once I had made up my mind:

1. To reactivate and reorganize every capability and
   asset, to recognize the therapy available in work,
   even the most menial housekeeping chores, to
   remember the need for fresh air exercise.
2. To hang on to basic values, but to honestly try to
   relate to a strange world—brutally impersonal at
   times, competitive, and dangerous.
3. To think about the thrust of God in the contemporary.
4. To remember the happy things.
5. To live and think creatively as though I really
   believed those words chiseled in gray marble
   there near the grave: "And all things, whatsoever
   ye shall ask in prayer, believing, ye shall receive"
   (Matt. 21:22).

6. To take a long look to the next generation; specifically, to know my grandchildren better, but—just as important—never to forget that they need to know me better, and their grandfather through me.
7. To quit striving! To live on top of despair, for "the Lord . . . will give grace and glory" (Ps. 84:11).

In such deeply personal moments, one remembers people, places, impressions. I remember the last time I saw my mother.

The loss of weight, ingeniously camouflaged, was nevertheless apparent. Mama wore a fancy cook apron over her next-to-best dress as she and Papa stood on the porch of their white frame cottage. Her silvery hair, rolled in those old-fashioned flat metal curlers the night before, was fluffy around her face. Although she had used her simple cosmetics carefully, the pain showed through in her eyes, and around her mouth, yet she greeted me the way she always did—happy and excited.

Inside, the table was set. The pink linen cloth and napkins, the crystal goblets always used for company, the pink rose china (not fine, but her best), the monogrammed silver I had used all my life—everything had been planned to make a perfect picture. The fried chicken, the delectable lemon pie showed that she had worked hard to get ready for our visit. There was no lowering of standards.

On the living room table, she had arranged a crystal bowl of her early spring roses.

I was to remember later the many painful steps she had taken to create such a scene for us. She had not forgotten the extra touches. Nothing of beauty was ever too much trouble, for she never counted, she said, the steps nor the stitches for those she loved.

Only shortly after that evening came the anguishing call to return home at once. Coming home was different that time; I had never had such feelings before. But the aching fatigue, the unutterable pain had to be pushed back. There were things to be done for Mama, things that only I could do. I knew what she would want; I understood the proprieties. The affinity between us was still there. Over my first experience of grief, there was a hovering grace and, for Mama, an enveloping glory.

There are some who say that being a woman is a liability. I counter that, for to us has been given something that transcends fads and fashions, trends and movements, and all the flaunting banners of the relentless years. In my own mortality, I am sustained by those ennobling qualities of my mother's womanhood, the strength of her femininity, her self-giving creativity, her incredible threshold of pain, and—always—her enduring spirit for good. This, in the best sense, is what being a woman means.

And I know that I shall live again, someday, with grace and glory.

VIII

Look Out Another Window

"My heart and my soul and my body are important to me."

DINAH SHORE

IT SEEMED THE ONLY THING to do—have my hair frosted.

My daughter Helen said it would update me, and that's exactly what I needed. Of course, I knew that. It was a matter of image, the composite me, as well as of my reflection in the mirror.

"And why," she asked with a hint of exasperation, "don't you buy some new clothes? And wear pants suits like everybody else? They're so youthful, and your figure is still good."

(There was some comfort in the thought that my own child, one's severest critic, conceded the point about my figure, and that she did not add the devastating phrase, "for a woman of your age.")

In a jargon as foreign to me as a language course in college, she briefed me on meaningful relationships, relevance to contemporary thought, coping with life as it is, self-determination, encounters . . . "and for goodness' sake, Mother, try to be more flexible!"

Four walls will not contain this daughter of mine. Well

educated, a leader in her community, she is definitely a part of her world. To add that she has a brilliant mind, a directness in handling reality, and a full share of good common sense would justify her upbraiding me for my pride in her, and my respect. At times, however, her bounding energy tires me to the bone, and I have to admit to the generation gap.

She was right, naturally! To borrow a phrase from *Hello, Dolly*, the parade was passing me by; it was time to rejoin the human race. It would require courage, and perhaps a little flair, to take a good look at the world and, at the same time, appraise myself honestly.

Several busy, history-filled years had gone by since Dr. Raley's death, the world changing so fast that experts in every field were baffled about the future. "The best of times, the worst of times"—no one really knew. And I, whose roots were in another, slower time, found it difficult to adjust.

Even so, in a sudden spurt of determination one morning, I decided to "get with it," and follow Helen's advice. A lighter look, literally, and a lighter heart, figuratively, were worth a try. To decide on something new, even something a bit out of character, would break the pattern. What I had in mind was a brighter perspective for what lay ahead.

Friends encouraged me in this new venture, as trivial and giddy as it seemed. "You've got years ahead of you"— now that was a choice compliment, though somewhat modified by, "look as young as you can. . . ." And so the appointment was made.

The frosting was now in progress, and I was absolutely numb with anxiety over the outcome. Daring a glance in the mirrors surrounding me, I had to relax and resign myself to whatever fate would work out. It's a beginning, I thought—an effort toward something different. As the young would say, I was trying to shape up.

To my dismay, the beauty shop was crowded; it was a regular field day. There was no place for privacy, for sorting one's thoughts on the relevance of hair-frosting to the new and meaningful relationships I was to pursue.

"My mother had her hair frosted once. She just loved it," my dryer-neighbor shouted from under the inferno of her hood, "and you know, it really made a new woman out of her." My encourager, by now attracting attention, reported further that her mother was actually enjoying life.

Indeed! A new woman—that's for me! But why? For how long?

I was unnerved with apprehension and shock at my own daring.

"You'll look beautiful!" Another contribution to my morale came from a mirrored reflection along the battery of dressing tables. Trying not to look grim, I acknowledged this boost with a tentative smile.

By now, the dryer-voice was on her way, waving to everybody and saying that it was her birthday and that her husband was taking her out to dinner, that she had to hurry to pick up her dress at the cleaners—also the babysitter—and that she would see us. Confident, vibrant, like my daughter, she exuded youthful joy in living every moment.

So different from mine was that perspective, that view from another vantage point. It was nice to think about.

In my reading the night before (little of which I had understood) Marshall McLuhan had made it very plain that

the merging, whirling worlds of contemporary living will
have no place for the old-fashioned (not his word, exactly)
with a fixed point of view. People had to be flexible. I was
trying.

Further reading that women over forty years of age are
more vital to the times than ever before had heartened me.
I was reminded that being female and forty is a totally
different experience from what it had been just ten years
ago. I already knew that; my concern was for the second
forty years. I hoped that, given health, they could be
potentially the best, most productive part of life.

I had read somewhere that women, if they chose, could
be free from convention—no strings attached. Daringly
dangerous, I thought, and certainly not for me. But, to
continue, they could be free from home and family
responsibilities and think of themselves first. It all seemed
disconcerting to me that the glib social engineers, predict-
ing trends for the future, were inclined to scrap many of
the values and priorities so important to me.

In such a situation, how could I turn any proverbial
corners, turn my life around, or at least look at life from
another angle? Was it too late? Way past time? Was I so
inhibited by an image that I could not move past attending
proprieties? Was I too bound by personal tastes that
dictated in no uncertain terms that the new was not for
me?

I wondered about my possibilities, in time and energy,
and about whether I wanted to explore personal and
professional options. And I remembered the first time I
had thought about such an idea. . . .

It had been one morning, in our first retirement year, as
my husband and I had had our coffee there on the porch.

Without even leading up to it, he had said, "Why don't you start a piano class?"

That's exactly what I had done! My old piano degree had had to be freshened up a bit, but had still worked. I couldn't have known then that this would meet a need later in my life, or that it would become such a source of meaningful dividends. It had just seemed very logical. Dr. Raley had begun another career, that of religious journalism, and was well into his column-writing for several hours a day. Why not try it? Housework was minimal. Entertaining was much simpler than it had been in the President's home. Our children were busy with their own lives. Life, generally, was easy. The world looked good. I still think of the brightness. . . .

How the mind wanders when ticking off times past. A hair dryer is good for that. One remembers the oddest things, the long-ago details more vivid now. . . .

I had hardly worn the new off my wedding trousseau when I sat myself down one day, if a bit late, to read a book called *Marriage Manual for Ministers' Wives*. The shock of what I had gotten myself into and what was expected of me lingers and frightens me to this day.

There it was in print that a woman really needs two husbands—in one person, of course—one to love her and one to support her. (I wonder what marriage counselors would say to that in these days. There would be two strikes against such an idea being taken seriously in today's society—the man shortage and women's freedom to say, "who needs a husband anyway?") But if a woman needs two husbands, the book said, a husband needs four wives! She must be (1) a woman of charm and culture, (2) an intelligent leader in a democratic society, (3) an efficient careerist, and (4) the maker of a successful home, which would, of course, include children.

Furthermore—and this I took seriously—the woman I was to become might not change the world, but could almost turn it over if I made up my mind to do it.

And so, although I was very young, I tried to be those four wives to my husband, whose career was mine too. I was loved for trying. In a demanding daily regimen, I became a composite of all those things expected of my life. Little bits of me fitted into the pattern of self-improvement. Miserably failing at times, often vulnerable to resentment, criticism and scrutiny, I was deeply, richly rewarded. There are no regrets. . . .

"Time to take your hair down! You're just sittin' on 'ready.'" The abrasive interruption to my sentimental reverie annoyed me, although I was in a hurry to get out of the place. I had been flicking through the pages of a woman's magazine there on the table, halfway reading the so-called counseling column. To the most intimate details, an ailing marriage was being analyzed and passed around for consumption. The article reported that seminars are filled with anxious women who vacillate between the good wife image and the yearning for freedom.

I accepted such crusades for marital happiness as reflective of a trend, and although somewhat offended by the therapeutic procedures suggested, I was heartily assured by the young writer that society could not survive without marriage and the family. With such a concession to an older woman's persuasion, I was not inclined to discount whatever good came from current research; rather, I was just slightly amused, and a little indignant over the gullibility of those involved. The basic element as I had known it—love—was missing in the entire discussion.

While the beauty operator arranged my hair, I sat wondering: If I had my life to live over, would I do the same? Be the same? How would I have fared in these times, speaking the language of love, absorbing the tensions, reaching past the pressures?

Perhaps I was not ready to venture into the unfamiliar, to deflect those memories, now as ethereal as some melody by Debussy. Could I look up and beyond the walled-in privacy that held me together? Could I diminish that difference between the limited confines of loneliness and the horizons of thought and energy and involvement, and still be the person I am?

At close range now, I could see possibilities.

As I gathered up my purse, my needlepoint, and my new self, I decided that I liked what I saw in the mirror. Really, I couldn't believe such "transformation." With a new boldness and an effort to the prescribed flexibility, I was ready for some kind of an embarcation. Just one backward glance would quiet me before launching, just one moment to get my bearings, to lift my face and my new courage to life around me.

"You'll love it!" my new friend had said.

Flinging inhibitions to the wind, at least symbolically, I assumed a new stance and made some new plans.

As I walked out of the shop, the Chapel clock reminded me that it was time to put my mind on Margaret Jane's piano lesson. I thought that just a hint of rubato on the third page of the Schumann might define the theme better, and I wondered if Margaret Jane would like my hair.

I held on tight, getting used to my "new" and unfamiliar self, as I drove along West University Street . . . toward another perspective.

My priority was to sort out the past, and never to forget the plus factors in my life. At the same time, I was to clean and polish those long-neglected windows that had limited my vision for too long. Some needed immediate attention. Had I waited too long to discard impediments to a better life? Perhaps it was time to build brand new windows— wider, higher, more receptive to new friends and experiences and to the expanding world.

A new enthusiasm, a spirited energy made the rest of the day go well. There was an excitement about planning for tomorrow, a sense of fulfillment even in the mundane details of life. I felt adequate, in control; by such a simple decision, I had thrown away the burden of futility.

A friend had observed recently that I was happy and didn't know it. . . . No, not happy—not ever again in the ecstasy of young love, nor in the deep and caring kind that grows through the vicissitudes of life together. But there was a sense of blessedness, of well-being, an assurance that nothing would ever be so hard again, nothing would ever hurt so acutely.

It had taken time, but the view was better now, brighter than it had been in a long time.

I have always liked mornings. From the desk where Dr. Raley did so much of his work, looking north through a wide picture window, I am impelled into this precious time of every new day. Sitting there, I sometimes remember a prayer-poem I used to quote to my class of college girls:

Let there be many windows in your soul,
That all the glory of the Universe
May beautify it . . .

At certain times as I sit at the window, I can see my reflection in the brightness of the morning. For me, even on a gray day, I would like it to be that of mature courage, of a valiant spirit, and of a splendor called faith.

A new woman, indeed!

Let me look in the mirror, first, then out the window!

IX

Faith So Strong
It Is Decisive

"Personal faith is the living tissue of conviction."

JOHN WESLEY RALEY

INDECISION, I AM TOLD, is one of the first signs of mental illness. It is indicative, at least, of a certain disorientation, to say nothing of one's age showing. Even the most trivial this-or-that gets all out of proportion sooner or later: Do I like this color? Shall I wear the new dress or save it for ————? Shall I eat my dinner now or later? Is this a good subject, or maybe that one would be better? Shall I clean house or go shopping? Change the oil today or tomorrow? Shall I go on a trip or stay home?

"Well, decide something!" Dr. Raley would say. "Do you or don't you? Make up your mind, and let all eventualities fall into place. And when you decide, let me know!" Then he would add, "You have to decide the main issue. It may be right or it may be wrong, but you have to take that responsibility." He meant it. "Who has time to wait for the perfect answer anyway?"

I have learned from many widow friends that they have the same problem with indecision that I have. Widows, particularly those who feel afraid to change their lifestyles, often face the most basic choices. What lies ahead depends on many factors. Where shall I live? Should I move out of the family home? A smaller place to maintain? An apartment? Where would I be safe? Should I stay where my friends are? What about church, clubs, a retirement group? Do I have some commitments I would have to give up? Should I move closer to the children, or move in with them? Would a change create more problems than it would solve?

Younger widows with children have as a first priority the well-being of the family unit—the children's schools, friends, influences in their lives, and most of all their sense of permanence. Although young families accept mobility as a way of life these days, there seems to be an increasing tendency toward settling down, developing helpful relationships with neighbors, friends, or possibly nearby relatives.

Then, there is the matter of just plain economics, including security costs, payments on house and car, health care, insurance, maintenance, an emergency fund. For many, the necessity for cutting corners is a very real factor.

What about a job? To make enough to support myself and the children?

What qualifications do I have?

Can I get into some kind of an in-service program?

How can I adjust to employment, an eight-to-five schedule, and still care for home and children?

What about my health—physical and emotional?

Isn't the routine of having to meet the world at a certain time each day better than aimlessness?

What about prospects for the future? Goals?

Dare I hope that there will be something better ahead?

Such questions are the very elements of everyday living; they are very real and, in varying degrees and circumstances, common to every woman on her own. There are always decisions to make.

When I was first widowed, every decision seemed contingent on another. What should I decide first? The chain reaction of ambivalence became so tangled that I finally wrote down such ridiculous steps as:

1. Decide on ———when I get a go-ahead through ———.
2. Then, if ———comes through, go this way: ———.
3. Provided the letter comes today, decide to do this: ———.
4. In case of a deadline, call, or decide some alternative before committing ———.
5. If———suggests, try another direction, but keep option open if ———.

It got to the point that I was ruining everything with ramifications, qualifications, "what-ifs." I always wanted time to think. If I arrange the pink roses in the crystal vase, would they show off well here or there? How about the silver bowl? Dare I try that new recipe? Or maybe I'd better stick to the old one. If I did this, what about that? Should I call or not call?

This had to stop! It was all so childish, and I recognized this indecision as a kind of evasiveness. It was a sort of mental trial and error, a debilitating vacillation. In the process of coping, I was aware of directions I could take that could either destroy or strengthen. I must learn which to follow; I must learn some degree of conviction. Yes, conviction. I positively would not give in to a poverty of either mind or spirit. Nancy Kissinger said problems existed to be solved, and she just may be right. I had to put my mind on that.

Although it meant a long time in the stage of writing down the pros and cons of situations in neat columns, I came through several years of making decisions on my own. I developed some confidence in my own capability to make major decisions if necessary.

But the loose ends of life still bother me. I want everything put together, all decisions made, all choices clear. This, as unrealistic as it is, has kept me striving toward some grounding, some assurance of the fact of faith.

I read Eileen Guder's book, *The Many Faces of Friendship*, and I couldn't question her affirmation that, "To Christians, death is the fundamental of one's faith." I needed to read about such an experience; this articulate writer had gone through the loss of a little daughter just before the onslaught of leukemia took her young husband. She writes of faith that came first through others, the touch of friends. Reading that, I was reminded of William James's statement: "Our faith is someone else's faith." By now, I know exactly what that meant. Through all the decisions I had to make without Dr. Raley, it was the awareness of his strong faith that sustained me. With this on my mind one day, I took the time to look up some translations in the Bible collection he had left so carefully intact there by his desk. Three small memo sheets fell out of *The New English Bible*.

In atrocious handwriting, almost illegible, he had listed some ideas, just words and phrases, for an article he was writing.

Here they are: "cutting finality, actuality of life, heavenly observance [I wonder what he was thinking], staying power, a saga of faith, antiseptic vigor [what on earth!], moral ferocity, petty pretention and cheap insincerity, ruthless love. . . ." And then, "faith so strong it is decisive," and, as a summation, "Personal faith is the living tissue of conviction."

The phrase, "living tissue" haunts me. Were those ideas slashed out on paper just about the time he thought he was recovering from the first surgery? He had listened carefully as the doctors explained all the pathological tests and examinations, even the findings after the second surgery. He had asked questions about living cells, living tissue.

Knowing him so well, and having been so close to him during those distraught days, I can follow the logic of his thinking. It was now that he needed his strongest resource, the "living tissue" of his conviction. In time, he rallied his personal faith to accept the inevitable.

A faith so strong—this is what he left me. It has worked in all the decisions, even those that seemed trivial, as well as in all those frightening contingencies. And it must be translated into the simplest lived-with handling of ordinary things, as well as into the maturing grace of experience.

A young faculty wife will never know the comfort she gave me one day when she interviewed me for a campus publication. There was a brief lapse in the questioning as we sat there in the Chapel. I must have given way to a momentary sadness; I remember looking around just in time to catch a shaft of morning sun through the brilliant colors of my favorite window. My thoughts lingered there for a while, then I heard my friend say, almost in a whisper: "What faith builds cannot be destroyed."

Here was the courage I needed to go on, to deal with the "loose ends" of my life. I had waited so long to come up from the escape of unreality. Now there was evidence of a vital, living faith. In different ways, others have felt it, and have been inspired by it. We have all, at various times, reached over or through some impasse to achieve, at last, a plateau of personal faith. Perhaps this is what C. S. Lewis meant by the "golden apple of selfhood."

I have been heartened by examples of many who have been forced to make decisions about "the way ahead," "the rest of my life," "on my own"—in faith. The younger-than-middle-aged matron—charming, attractive, a superb hostess—was stunned by the sudden death of her husband, a prominent lawyer. With dignity and flair, and with no hint of false pride, she went to work immediately in the elegant dress shop she had always patronized. Now she models originals for her clientele, most of them her friends.

The young war widow, whose Air Force husband had been shot down in Vietnam, was determined to maintain their home for her two small children. Investing the insurance, she became interested in business and banking. Now her cashier's window hours coincide with the children's school schedule. They are going to make it.

A legend in her time is the fragile "best cook in town," who was widowed and left with a small son to raise when she was a very young woman. With amazing spirit and energy, she built a business on what she knew best—cooking—and the world still beats a path to her door. Neither age nor physical disability keeps her from filling the orders for cakes and pies, casseroles, cookies, and fancy party food. Her cookbooks, selling at five dollars each, help to support her favorite charity.

These are profiles of my friends who have made it through on their own faith, their own conviction.

And then, there's Jo. . . .

With a hop, skip, and a jump, she flits around town, never to lose a minute of living. I had tried some three months to reach her in her downtown apartment, just missing her between a trip to New York, an early summer jaunt to Colorado and, of all things, a Retired Association bus trip to historic shrines in the South. Later there was a sentimental journey to the jubilee celebration of her sorority on the campus of the eastern university where her husband, a professor of law, had died many years ago.

At long last, I met Jo one August morning over the card catalogue at the public library. She had walked across the park, parasol atop her slender, agile figure, dressed for the day in the smart summer cotton with white accents.

"I've been trying to reach you all summer," I whispered. "Can you visit just a minute?"

"Oh, yes! I do have a deadline, however. You see, I'm to take some lunch to a friend just out of the hospital . . . I'll have to pick up my car. What a fine morning to be out! I've already been downtown shopping. . . . Tell me, what's on your mind?"

"I've just got to ask you something!"

"Well, I simply cannot stand the curiosity! Let's get back behind the stacks."

And so, in subdued voices, we talked in the most personal way about life and about how we had made those decisions that took us through the widowhood we had both experienced. I needed all the encouragement that she could give me.

"You mean so much to all of us who have loved you . . . tell me, Jo, have you had, in all these widowed years, a sort of magic formula, a creed or a philosophy that has carried you past retirement when everybody else is sitting quietly in a corner? In the first place, how did you survive the death of your husband? You were so young. . . ."

Across her face there was just a tiny quiver. Unfalling tears filled her eyes behind her smart-looking glasses. She told me something of those eight blissful years of marriage, the two little girls, the happy faculty-wife status, the position of sorority advisor, the prospects for the future.

"I came out of it because he would have wanted it that way. I could cry later, and once, after a few weeks, I did cry it out. I found a secluded spot in the country where the children and I had found some warmth. I wept quietly, all by myself, all afternoon. Then the children came looking for me, and I couldn't cry any more. Later, when we returned to my childhood home, I didn't want my mother and father to see me cry. . . ."

"But, Jo, the *joie de vivre*—it never seems to dispel. You spread it around to all of us. You are alert to every contact, every opportunity. You read all the books, you see all the shows, you entertain, you do your church work. How did this come to be?"

More than economics was involved, she said, although that was a sizeable factor. She had had to meet the challenge of raising and educating two children. With the help of family and friends, she had reactivated her confidence in herself, her zeal and enthusiasm for life and people. Her indomitable will had taken over.

She recounted the courage it had taken to buy a completely new wardrobe of clothes, knowing for certain that she should have saved the money for the children, but considering it an investment. Qualifying for a teaching career, she had set a tenure record, and had become the favorite teacher of hundreds in our town—a welcome guest for every occasion.

We finished our conversation as I drove her back to her apartment. It was then that we spoke of our common creeds, our basic Christian faith, of our belief that if we did our best we would be sustained by that strength in the ultimate will of God. Only in such trust could there be a positive outlook on life.

About Jo there was a radiance, a shining through, because she believed. There was a normal wholehearted-ness, but never a hint of abrasive piosity; rather, it was a matter of good cheer, of decisive, assertive hope. Jo had no dull moments. Her telephone calls made our days, and to be her guest at some special occasion was considered the highlight of the season.

I shall always remember this valiant friend who had walked the lonely road with such grace and bearing and, always, joy, because, as she said, she didn't want to miss anything. "And my routine," she said, "is exceedingly pleasant."

Could it be that I was trying to learn this when I was a very young minister's wife in a brief pastoral experience before coming to the university? We had hardly unpacked our few belongings when the invitation was extended to me from the Rebekah Sunday School Class (the grandmothers) to attend their meeting, and "would I bring a few devotional thoughts?" I felt so honored; in a way, this was my first introduction to church work.

In all the wisdom of my nineteen years, I talked to the Rebekah Sunday School Class about: "Weeping may endure for a night, but joy cometh in the morning" (Ps. 30:5). What made me choose such an unlikely text I'll never know. It was probably the very words, the beauty and the cadence; or perhaps I was thinking of my mother and of the many times she would say that worries were much worse at night, that things always looked better in the morning.

Years later, I read Emily Dickinson:

> Will there really be a morning?
> Is there such a thing as day?
> Could I see it from the mountains
> If I were as tall as they?

This is why I like mornings! I am told, however, that many women who live alone dread waking up to another day; they hope to prolong the effect of a sleeping tablet as long as possible. Not I! And that's something good going for me. To me, morning is a listening time, a sorting-out time, and a deciding time.

When I checked on another early riser, several months now since the long and tragic vigil she had kept, I was reassured by the confidence in her voice, the wonder of her faith. "Oh, Helen," she said, "I am at peace about Bob, and about me." She had moved in and through the very eye of the storm, sustaining a full measure of pain and anguish, and had found the "I will be with thee" (Isa. 43:2) there all the time.

I thought about Leslie Weatherhead's contention that in God's will our conflicts will be resolved, and that peace of mind comes progressively as we go through certain stages and choices and decisions. This, I decided, may well be my special adventure in living again.

My husband had written it down firmly with his smudgy old pen—"a faith so strong it is decisive," and "the living tissue of conviction." He had held on to that. And I think he knew that I would grow toward such assurance.

"Only by faith," he had told me in love.

X

The Smallest Star

"Alas for him who never sees
The stars shine through the cyprus trees."

WHITTIER

I LEARNED FROM FRAN the comfort of finding one's own little star.

Among my friends, Fran is a pint-sized dynamo, one of those can-do women who set out to win wars. Through political channels—from committee chairperson to precinct delegate, then on to city council member, this astute businesswoman has impressive influence not only in our town, but all over the state. Tireless in her crusade for better housing, better schools, better streets, care for the aging, and representation for all people, she is completely available to every need. Her black, snapping eyes, her bounding energy, and her gift for speechmaking are all to her advantage. Besides all this, she runs a real estate business, maintains a home, and enjoys life.

I don't see Fran often, but over the telephone one night she brightened my life considerably. . . .

"To the State Convention? All those women?" I demurred. It was a prestigious organization, and I was flattered by the invitation to speak at their annual banquet in Oklahoma City.

"What do you want me to talk about?" I asked tentatively.

"Something women would like!" was her immediate response.

"Fran, after all this time, I seem to have so little to say. You'll have to let me think about it. . . . For now, let me read you something; it's so poignantly beautiful, it hurts." My heart skipped a beat and I waited for a little control. "Try to know how I feel."

I read Thomas John Carlisle's little poem:

> Because I live alone
> I leave a light
> To help me find my way
> Back home by night.
> But if I could
> Walk home again with you,
> To bring us safe,
> The smallest star would do.

We were both quiet for a moment, and then my friend said, "I would like for you to talk about stars."

To explain, Fran told me about her special little star.

A few years before, bereft of both father and mother, she, an only child, had faced the realization that she was the last of her family. On the night her mother slipped away, she had walked off into the farthest and darkest corner of the backyard and had looked over the tops of the trees to find her little star, the smallest one, shining pink like a little sequin tucked away in the corner of the heavens. Her mother had always told her to look for the smallest star, that it would always be there like "a diamond in the sky."

And so, no matter how difficult the going, how disillusioning the human factor, how grim the world of politics, that little pink star has given Fran the courage to keep on. It has symbolized a faith that, in the words of Robert Frost, "asks of us a certain height."

The Bible says that "the morning stars sang together" (Job 38:7). My friend Dr. Angell writes of the drama of the night sky, when "star rises after star"—always a study for the imaginative mind, the curious spirit, and the lonely heart. To men of simple faith, stars of antiquity were signs of the times, portents of the future. To modern men of science, stars are guideposts, whether for stabbing the sky with powerful missiles or slicing the seas with the most sophisticated naval equipment.

In one's efforts toward faith, "a star to steer her by" is life's only invariable. It charts one through the dark and fearsome passages of reality, shining brightest when needed most. And in times of crisis, in periods of crushing sorrow, "He healeth the broken in heart, and bindeth up their wounds. He telleth the number of the stars; he calleth them all by their names" (Ps. 147:3–4).

It was the great German philosopher, Immanuel Kant, who perceived and expounded that the two most astounding facts of the universe are the starry heavens and the moral law in man. Much later, the renowned Dorothy Thompson added a classic, much quoted affirmation—that the Christian ethic, the scientific spirit, and the Rule of Law constituted the guiding philosophy of Western civilization. From the fixedness of these verities, these invariables, man triumphs over circumstances of despair.

And so, I talked about stars that night at the State Convention—how we, even we of little faith, can each in our own way reflect the beauty and guidance of the smallest star. In all the overwhelming changes of contemporary society, we have to know for sure that some things remain—the eventual triumph of good, the stirrings of love in the human heart, the indomitable spirit of man. Like stars in constancy, in continuity, those qualities of grace, integrity, industry, and innate goodness provide a way toward faith. The physical passes, the spiritual endures. We can know. We cannot live without knowing.

I was to learn this through many lessons. . . .

"It's for you." Somebody handed me the Volunteer Desk telephone.

"Can you come to the second floor?" a composed voice asked. "We need you."

"I'm on my way," I said.

The head nurse was waiting. She came from behind her desk to speak quietly: "It's the terminal case in 210. We didn't know it would be so soon. The family would like to go to the Chapel. Will you stay with them awhile?"

The Chapel in our hospital is just a room, but a very special one, away from the corridor traffic and waiting rooms and yet accessible. A simple sign, "Chapel," identifies the door. All faiths are represented there by appropriate symbols, all given as memorials. There is a burnished brass candelabrum, seven-branched, given by a family who lost a little girl. An elaborately bound Bible rests on a carved stand. The Book of Common Prayer is near; an ornate silver cross on a velvet-colored pedestal honors a family with deep roots in Lebanon. On one wall, a contemporary work of hammered silver depicts The Last Supper. A sofa, a desk with soft light, and comfortable chairs complete the furnishings.

The family and I walked to the elevator. "You will know what to say," the nurse had told me.

I honestly tried. It was hard; my own grief came back. And I remembered similar situations, even back when I was very young, when I had tried to help. The phrases of comfort seemed meaningless. Perhaps silence would be better. . . .

"We are never ready," was a beginning. "Sorrow comes to all of us. You will not go through this alone. I know that. And you have so many friends. How can I help you now?"

I kept trying, but nothing sounded right. If I just sat quietly, simply stayed close. . . . I knew it was no time to say that life.must go on.

And then, in a strange way, I seemed to hear Dr. Raley quoting those Whittier lines:

> Yet Love will dream, and Faith will trust,
> (Since He who knows our need is just,)
> That somehow, somewhere, meet we must.

All the time I was thinking: if we could only look over, or away, or perhaps beyond, to the ultimate will of God, the unending glory, our questions would be answered, but for now the human heart cries out the world's oldest question, "Why?" In our limitation we see "through a glass darkly"; we see just a small segment of the whole span. Only by faith, Dr. Raley always said, can we be sure of the perfect circle, the endless joy. Would he know now about the farthest star, the smallest?

I remembered my beautiful friend, silver-haired, brown-eyed Arlene, who really believes that, in the realms of the eternal, life will be complete. She and Basil had been married over fifty years—a deep and abiding marriage—when she lost him to a massive coronary. Since then, she has become more and more sure of the continuity of life. In a very literal way, she plans for reunion. The promise of a higher sphere, mystical and supernatural though it will be, helps to assuage her present grief, her lonely waiting.

If only I could say something like that right now. My mind had wandered briefly. It was time to suggest to the family that I could help with telephone calls. Would anyone like coffee, I wondered, or would they like me to call their minister?

Soon the shock began to dispel. There was a lifting up of tear-streaked faces to get on with the practical matters. I walked out to the car with them and tried to say what I had heard my husband speak so softly to the bereaved, "Grief opens doors to others; just walk through them. God love you."

It was a Sunday morning in June—the twenty-third, our wedding anniversary. Nine years had passed since Dr. Raley's death.

Thinking of the hundreds of Sunday mornings I had heard him speak on joyous, triumphant faith, I decided this was the morning to listen to some of his sermon tapes, all catalogued now. Sometime in the future, I had always said, not now. But today was different. Carefully I threaded the tape into the machine and started the motor, then sat quietly as the familiar voice began. . . .

One remembers little bits of time, little pieces of living. On the morning I first heard that sermon we had been running late. Dr. Raley was to have been guest minister for an early church service. I can see him now as he sat down at his desk, began to make hurried notes on sheets of old stationery—a sort of beige color, just scraps—which he folded into neat, pocket-sized pages. And then, with his stubby old Parker pen, he had written down an outline, each heading with its subpoints numbered 1, 2, 3, then strange hieroglyphics which must have been an illustration, and then the first line of a poem.

He had laid aside the neat, perfectly typed sermon notes he had planned. And then, typically, he had shoved the scribbled notes down into his coat pocket, put on his hat, and said, "Let's go!"

Now, remembering, I could see that batch of notes clearly. I wondered if I could find them; were they still in one of those old notebooks I had not dared to open?

Quickly, I walked across the room to the wall of books, his working library. Taking down the five old, black leather loose-leaf notebooks, I found what I was looking for—three pages, beige, pocket-sized, held together with a rusty paper clip.

Here were his notes on "Ways to Faith," just as he had left them—the terrible handwriting, the smudged words, some scratched through and all blurred by that leaky old pen—the workings of the mind behind the powerful voice on the tape:

John 4:5–30, 39–42

This story, artfully told, reveals all the factors of a great drama. The characters, the situation, the relationships were fitted into a perfect plot to evoke the response planned by the great Playwright. The tensions of the times were fully reflected. [The next sentence was partially obscured, but there was something about social, racial, and religious pressures.]

After grasping the situation, definite principles emerge to answer the question used as a subject, "Ways to Belief in God through Christ" . . . Why and how do we believe?

I.   Because others believe. Pages from one's own life reveal those personalities and influences leading to belief.

II. We reason our way to Faith through philosophy and logic. . . . Descartes, Napoleon. . . . Illustration from *Gone With the Wind* when Rhett says to Scarlett—"Is it a person or a thing you are hunting, Honey?" "I don't know," she replied. "I really don't know."

III. The Impact of the Person of Jesus. The gate is personal belief. When we see Him in Divine confrontation, we believe. It happens. It is personal. It is face to face.

Because I had read over and over, and had been told, that the search for God begins at the point of deepest and darkest need, the end of a known way, I could understand the sermon better now than I had on the day it was delivered. I could accept the mystery that death is just a closer horizon, and that somewhere the stars are bright with the assurance of immortality.

A page of recent reading provides an apt description of the universal experience of grief—the going down into it, the coming up through it toward assuagement, then triumph. In describing his and Julie's anguish through the bizarre episodes of Watergate, David Eisenhower wrote a letter of concern to his father-in-law, Richard M. Nixon, in which he enclosed this quotation from George Eliot:

> There is no despair so absolute as that which comes the first moment of our first great sorrow, when we have not yet known what it is to have suffered and be healed, to have despaired and recovered hope.

Although the context is unfamiliar to me, I believe the words speak with clarity and affirmation to all who grieve.

I am a year stronger now, every year a little stronger. I can feel it.

It is summer again, the morning bright. The sweetgums

and maples have survived first a searing summer of drought, then a bitter and icy winter, and now are in full leaf, shading the yard. Bright red geraniums defy the terrapins—strange wobbly creatures, one still marked with red fingernail polish brushed on years ago by Dr. Raley and our small granddaughter. The Queen Elizabeth roses are blooming; the begonias, fragile but growing; and the petunias, a new color this year, are banked in my mother's fernery.

Yesterday, an old graduate dropped by to see me. He was from the class of '55, a successful businessman now, older and somewhat broader—but I would have known Chuck anywhere. He wanted to talk about his college days: the parties, the pranks (some fully revealed now), the games, the draft calls, the grade points, the loves, the hurts . . . and all the people. Together, we wondered about that throaty contralto who had sung "Autumn Leaves" with the Glee Club, and about the guy who was the best basketball player we ever had.

I think now about the continuity of life as I have known it through many college generations. This is the going on. As someone said upon Dr. Raley's death, "Helen, remember you still have the old students. . . ." It is in remembering, then, that I am heartened.

"What is your life like now?" Chuck asked.

"Oh, my life is full, so much to do, so much I'll never get it done."—I began to check the calendar. "It's Commencement time again. May, you know, is a month of music. From the Chapel I shall hear the arias, the piano concertos, the orchestras and chorales, the great organ sounds . . ."

The writing course I am taking excites me.

Volunteering at the hospital gives me the opportunity to serve.

A few house-bound friends say they need me.

I am rehearsing my pupils for their recital.

The correspondence continues as it always has.

House and yard, children and grandchildren (college age now!). I am involved, active, well, and life is good. I must keep trying!

These ten years have been marked by sudden, rapid changes in my personal world, and in life all around me. Man has walked on the moon; life on earth will never be the same. Because the world has changed so much, the woman alone must cope with unimagined vicissitudes. To maintain oneself is a challenge. It is in trying that we survive.

And in faith, those who have loved and have lost their love learn to live again—revitalized, reenergized into new patterns, and new ventures.

When there were no stars for me, my faith was often stricken by hurtful blows, by a sense of old values slipping away, by the realization of my own finitude. Gradually, I grew to know that there is life after death, that transcending love wanders through all the vistas of immortality, and that memories linger and bless through all the stretches of time and space.

Ahead are different days, days more precious because of those I have lived. With an unprecedented flexibility of schedule, I am involved with the list of "things to do" that is always on my desk. There is no ecstatic happiness, but rather a measure of contentment, a balance between obligatory demands and the pursuit of my own disciplines. Always with me is the thought that Dr. Raley was one of those people Thomas Wolfe described as having "the energy of joy and delight." And I can hear his voice even now—clear, resonant, timeless. I hear him finish the lines:

> Life is ever Lord of Death,
> And Love can never lose its own.